Praise for 1(

"With unflagging wit, unfailing insight, and light-hearted wisdom, Karl Keating has produced what can only be called a masterpiece. *1054 and All That* deserves a place on the shelf alongside the great Catholic raillery of figures like Belloc and Chesterton. Page after page, it's an utter delight."

Robert Royal, author of *A Deeper Vision: The Catholic Intellectual Tradition in the 20th Century*

"It takes a special gift to pen a work of ecclesiastical history that is pithy, informative, and truly funny. Karl Keating has that gift. Rarely is the Catholic Church's past rendered with such wry readability!"

Carl E. Olson, editor of *Catholic World Report*

"What would it feel like to read 2,000 years of Church history in 140 pages written by Monty Python or the editors of The Onion (the successor to *Punch*)? Like a hundred giggles and belly laughs. Like this book. Get it and read it before the Thought Police outlaw the remnants of permissible humor and history."

Peter Kreeft, author of *Ha!: A Christian Philosophy of Humor*

"This is the most enjoyable thing I've read since Bill Bryson's *A Walk in the Woods*."

Michael T. Cibenko, author of *Masaru*

"Karl Keating has been one of the treasures of Catholic apologetics. This is an immensely entertaining book about the history of the Church. You will laugh and perhaps learn something in the process!"

Austin Ruse, author of *Under Siege: No Finer Time to Be a Catholic*

"Karl Keating has done the impossible: he has made history fun. *1054 and All That* is full of witty insights and half-serious humor. I recommend this book to anyone who wishes a quick overview of Church history in the most delightful and winsome format possible."

Gary Michuta, author of *Revolt Against Reality*

"History or apologetics? Karl Keating's *1054 and All That* is a good-natured blend of both. Here's a witty, readable overview of two millennia that deflates hostile myths about the Church while setting the record straight by the clear light of fact."

Russell Shaw, author of *Eight Popes and the Crisis of Modernity*

"Buckle up! Keating's time machine will take you on a fast and funny ride through Church history, replete with heretics, heroes, and not a few hotheads."

Rose Sweet, author of *A Catholic Woman's Guide to Happiness*

"I chuckled on every page. With just the right amount of humor, and seasoned with his wit, Keating writes with a spritely style weaving together the key people and events covering two millennia. *1054 and All That* is an easy, informative, and delightful read."

Steve Ray, Bible teacher and Holy Land guide

"'Life is funny.' Everyone has made that observation. It follows that history—which is an accumulation of life's stories—must be funny, too. Karl Keating makes it so in this enjoyable little book. He brings out the comedy in the history of the Catholic Church, without sacrificing the fundamental accuracy of his narrative."

Philip Lawler, editor of *Diogenes Unveiled*

"*1054 and All That* is a masterpiece of Church history in Cliff Notes fashion. It seems an almost impossible feat to laugh about something so serious, but Keating manages to deftly align history with his wit."

Patti Maguire Armstrong, co-author of *What Would Monica Do?*

"This is a book whose appeal is twofold: it's light-hearted and offers an enlightening, reliable shortcut to mastering the basics of Church history. First-of-its-kind original."

Roger A. McCaffrey, editor of *And Rightly So: Selected Letters and Articles of Neil McCaffrey*

"Karl Keating sets about in *1054 and All That* to look back at the history of the Catholic Church: what we know, what we thought we knew, and what we did not know are all set forth with a good measure of mirth and humor. Enjoy this dive into the fascinating and inspiring history of Catholicism."

Fr. Gerald E. Murray, Pastor, Holy Family Church, New York City, and member of EWTN's Papal Posse

"G. K. Chesterton once wrote, 'It is the test of a good religion whether you can joke about it.' *1054 and All That: A Lighthearted History of the Catholic Church* makes the case for Chesterton. Here Karl Keating mixes up a spritzer of history and humor that will delight and edify readers. The pen-and-ink illustrations only add to the fun. Read and enjoy!"

Jeff Minick, author of *Amanda Bell*

1054 AND ALL THAT

1054
AND ALL THAT

A Lighthearted History
of the Catholic Church

KARL KEATING

ILLUSTRATIONS BY KURT R. KRESS

RASSELAS HOUSE

Published by Rasselas House
El Cajon, California
RasselasHouse.com

ISBN 978-1-942596-44-8 Ebook
ISBN 978-1-942596-43-1 Paperback
ISBN 978-1-942596-42-4 Hardback

Contents

A Fragmentary Preface   xi

Periods of Five Hundred Years   xiii

Period 1: The Early Years (A.D. 33 to 500)   1

Period 2: The Dark Ages (500 to 1000)   27

Period 3: The Middle Ages (1000 to 1500)   45

Period 4: The Modern Era (1500 Onward)   81

A Fragmentary Preface

Countless histories of the Catholic Church have been written by exalted historians, to instruct those in the pews on the story of their Church and, more urgently, to exalt the reputations of the historians. These efforts largely have failed, in both regards.

The historians are little remembered, and little of what they taught has been absorbed by Catholics who have read their histories or who have watched the motion picture adaptations.

The sad result is that most Catholics know only disjointed fragments of Church history, but that is better than not knowing anything at all. In these pages the disjointed fragments have been collected, for the recollection of said Catholics and for the instruction of The Next Generation.

Periods of Five Hundred Years

It is commonplace among historians to observe (as if no one else ever had made the observation) that Church history, like the history of the West in general, has fallen into periods of five hundred years or so.

First there were the first centuries, appropriately enough. They ended with the fall of Rome in 476, but we'll round it off to the year 500 to make the observation more observable.

The next five centuries were the Dark Ages. There wasn't much to see there. (There seldom is, in the dark.) That period ended in the year 1000, which was an even rounder number than 500, its roundness leading to all sorts of End of the World fears that would be topped only a millennium later with the Y2K kerfuffle, at which point nothing happened, just as nothing happened in 1000.[1]

The third period of five hundred years began with the transition from the Low Middle Ages to the High

---

1 Except that the Kingdom of Hungary was established, with Stephen I crowned on Christmas Day. Years later, he got promoted to saint.

Middle Ages (the thirteenth century, mostly) and then transitioned into the Renaissance, which was a high point for art, particularly if you lived in Italy, and a low point for political intrigue, particularly if you lived in Italy.

The fourth period of five hundred years began in 1500. This period is known as the Modern Era because anyone writing about it was born at the tail end of it and all such writers want to be considered Modern rather than, say, Middling, which was what the writers living in the Middle Ages were, or so people said.[2]

So much for the bird's-eye view. Now we turn to specifics of Catholic history, so far as they are understood or misunderstood—often enough, both at the same time.

---

2 Anyone born in the fifth period of five hundred years, which began in 2000, should not be writing history at all, not yet having lived through any.

Period 1

The Early Centuries

A.D. 33 to 500

Pentecost

The history of the Catholic Church begins with its founding by its Founder, who informed the first pope, Peter,[3] that he (the Founder) would build a Church. Always true to his word, since he himself was the Word, the Founder did so.

Called within a lifetime the Catholic Church because it was meant for men everywhere (*catholic* means *universal*, which in turn means *everywhere*), the Church came into the world on the Feast of Pentecost.

On its very first day the Church received three thousand new recruits. They became convinced by listening to the apostles preach in the listeners' own, disparate languages. This was before the advent of captioned videos, so everyone in Jerusalem was suitably impressed. Except for a Pharisee named Saul.

---

3 In this book future saints are not styled "St." because they weren't saints yet, not being dead, and even after their deaths the style continues, for consistency's sake. This saves much typographic space, so many such personages being mentioned. Besides, we're told that Saving Trees is a good thing, so there's that, if you're reading this as a printed book. If as an ebook, never mind.

Paul and Peter in Rome

The first great Christian missionary was Paul of Tarsus. His actual name had been Saul, but he changed it under an early version of the witness protection program.

Paul was noted for his many voyages to distant places. He seldom was able to convince any of his friends to accompany him because he had an unfortunate habit of getting shipwrecked.

He wrote epistles[4] to nascent Christian churches around the Mediterranean, often scolding them, often praising them. The scolding came naturally to Paul, inasmuch as he was brought up a Pharisee, and the praising came naturally to him also, because he was a model Christian.

Eventually Paul ended up in Rome as a prisoner. He was a Roman citizen, so his jailers had to treat him more tolerably than they treated other prisoners. He was allowed to have water. While in prison Paul met up with his long-time friend Peter, who was the earthly head of the Church. Peter had been hiding out in Rome, clandestinely tending to his flock, when someone finked on him. (Ever since, the surname Fink has held unsavory connotations.)

At length the jailers tired of having the two apostles as their charges. Peter was crucified upside down, and Paul lost his head. They were buried in different places. Paul was buried outside the walls of Rome, and Peter was buried smack dab beneath the centerline of the basilica that bears his name.

---

4 In our era usually called *letters*, but *epistles* is a more elevated term, and they are part of the Bible, which is the most elevated of books, so here they are called *epistles*.

John the Evangelist

The last apostle to die was John. He lived until the end of the first century, which meant he lived nearly as long as Bob Hope and Irving Berlin, but he was unaware of that because those two hadn't yet come to Ephesus, where John's tomb still may be found.

John is credited with writing the fourth Gospel and a trio of epistles and was known as "the disciple whom Jesus loved." (This is not to suggest that Jesus didn't love the other disciples.)

Whether John also wrote the book of Revelation is a matter of dispute. Some biblical scholars say that it and John's Gospel are so dissimilar in style that they could not have come from the same hand. Other scholars, not having confined themselves to reading the stilted prose of biblical journals, argue that writers alter their styles as they age and as they change genres, and so these scholars assert that John wrote Revelation as well as a Gospel.

A curious thing is that the first group of scholars insists that the writer of Revelation, like the writer of the fourth Gospel, was named John, though he was a different John. This reminds one of the famous remark that "Homer was not written by Homer but by another man of the same name."

After the Apostles

At the end of the first century the Apostolic Age ended because there were no more apostles. They all had gone to their respective rewards. The period that followed sometimes is called the Post-Apostolic Age, but more commonly it is called the second century. That century and the following ones were when the leading Christian writers were known as the Fathers of the Church. There is disagreement about when that age ended.

Traditionally, in the East, the end coincided with the death of John Damascene, who died in 749. In the West, also by tradition, the end coincided with the death of Isidore of Seville, who died in 636. This means there was a Fatherless vacuum of 113 years in the West, but no one noticed because Western society was in turmoil, and they had better things to do than to try to match the East Father for Father.

John the Baptist and Baptists

All of the earliest Christian writers were Catholics because all of the earliest Christians were Catholics. This is disputed by some modern-day Baptists, who hold that their denomination was founded by John the Baptist. This is a curious position because, if true, then their church was founded before the church founded by Christ.

John the Baptist, through the inconvenience of being murdered on orders from Herod, ended his missionary work about the time that Christ began his. It was some time later that Christ told Peter (whose original name had been Simon and whose new name, given to him by Christ, meant "Rocky") that "on this rock I will build [note future tense] my church" (Matt. 16:18).

In other words, any church founded by John the Baptist must have been founded before Christ had a chance to found his own. The two could not be the same institution. Modern-day Baptists would do better if they claimed that their denomination was founded in the seventeenth century by English Separatists, which in fact it was.

Ignatius of Antioch

One of the earliest Catholic writers was Ignatius of Antioch, who was martyred in Rome in 107. As he was being taken to Rome under guard, he wrote letters[5] to seven local churches that he passed along the way.

Among much else he said, Ignatius noted that the Eucharist is "the flesh of our Savior Jesus Christ, the flesh which suffered for our sins, the flesh which the Father in his goodness has raised again." This explicit and early affirmation of the Real Presence seems to be why there never has been a Baptist church named after Ignatius.

Justin Martyr

Among the earliest Christian writers (reminder: all of them were Catholics) were those known as the Catholic apologists. Not everyone nowadays knows the meaning of the term *Catholic apologist*. Here it is: a Catholic apologist is someone who goes around the country apologizing for being a Catholic.[6]

The earliest Catholic apologist was Justin Martyr. He was a philosopher who had been brought up a pagan. He experimented with various philosophies,

---

5 Not *epistles* because, as good as they were, they didn't make it into the Bible. Such are the breaks of divine inspiration.

6 This is a joke. If you didn't realize that at once, stop reading here. You won't understand the rest of this book.

found each one deficient, and became a Christian because only Christianity made sense. He was martyred for his troubles but got the last laugh because he became a saint.

Gnosticism

The early apologists had to refute anti-Christians of various sorts. Among the biggest opponents of Christianity were the Gnostics. The word comes from the Greek for "secret knowledge." Their knowledge was so secret that no one ever figured out exactly what they believed, including the Gnostics themselves.

This made Gnosticism attractive because, if you were a Gnostic, no one ever could prove that you believed incorrectly since no one ever could prove just what it was that Gnostics were supposed to believe. This is also why there were no Gnostic martyrs.

Gnosticism persisted for centuries, at times almost disappearing, at other times gaining strength. It has seen a resurgence in recent years. Most entertainers and nearly all television journalists are Gnostics: their beliefs, if any, are impossible to pin down.

Montanism

One of the earliest heresies was Montanism. It was known as an "enthusiastic movement" because its members were ancestors of the much-later Holy Rollers, except that they didn't handle snakes, which the Holy Rollers didn't either.

Montanists were certain that the Second Coming was coming soon. Their leaders were amateur mathematicians who read the Bible and purported to be able to compute the timing of the Last Day accurately. They were not as good at mathematics as they supposed, as their repeatedly computed days kept passing without incident.

Montanism was begun by a man who, in a wild coincidence, was named Montanus. (Centuries later, the sixteenth American president, in an equally wild coincidence, was named after the capital of Nebraska.)

Montanus, who lived in the second century, began his religious career as a self-declared prophet. He did not obtain the hearing he expected. Self-declared prophets seldom do, there being so many of them. He upped the ante and declared he was the Paraclete promised by Christ. This got people's attention.

Montanus began a speaking tour of Phrygia, which is said to have been named after its insalubrious climate, and soon won disciples, in particular two wealthy ladies, Maximilla and Prisca, who deserted their husbands to follow Montanus, thus setting a precedent that would be seen in much later religious movements.

Maximilla tried to prophesy on her own, saying, "After me the end will come," except that after her end it didn't. (Louis XV was more prescient, unfortunately, when he said something similar.) Montanism continued to be a problem for centuries, though Montanus himself didn't, as one might expect.

Victor I

Not long after Montanus passed from the scene, the bishop of Rome, Pope Victor I, declared that a different heretic, called Polycrates of Ephesus, had earned excommunication for being a public nuisance. This was the earliest recorded occasion of a pope issuing a disciplinary ruling regarding someone living far from Rome. It would not be the last occasion. It might not even have been the first, since most early records of such things don't seem to have been recorded, but Victor gets the credit. Such are the breaks of history, as every historian knows.

Victor found himself dealing with yet another heretic, a man named Eleutherius. He was a wealthy resident of Byzantium who had apostatized in a recent persecution. He came to Rome, a city where he was not known, to hide his shame. He was found out anyway. He tried to excuse himself by saying that in denying Christ he had not denied God because Christ was not God but merely the highest of all of God's creatures.

This did not sit well with Victor, who excommunicated Eleutherius, who refused to recant. Eleutherius began his own sect and deliberately filled it with logicians, mathematicians, and scientists. They studied not only the Bible but such Greeks as Euclid, Galen, and Aristotle. They were smart people who were too smart for their own good, and in a few decades the sect disappeared.

Manichaeism

In the next century, the third, things began to become troublesome. There arose yet another sect, that of the Manichaeans, and that one, unlike the sect of Eleutherius, lasted well more than a thousand years, proving that longevity in error depends on more than just having a roster of logicians, mathematicians, and scientists. The Manichaeans appeared under many titles in later years, such as Bougres, Cathars, and Albigenses—and that was just in the Middle Ages.

The founder of Manichaeism (in another of those wild coincidences) was a man called Mani. He was born in Persia and deliberately founded his new religion. It was intended to incorporate all of the wisdom of all of the world's religions.

For Mani there had been three great religious leaders in history: Christ, Zoroaster, and Buddha. The problem with them was that they only preached, never wrote. Mani would fix that by writing, which he considered an effective means of communicating his thoughts. It worked. More than a century later, for example, Augustine, for a time, was won over to Manichaeism by virtue of the heretic's writings.

Mani did not scruple to borrow from lesser religious leaders too, and, like Montanus, he concluded that he himself really was the Paraclete. As with Montanus, this tactic got people's attention. Mani and Montanus are credited with having invented the Art of Self Promotion.

Origen

Origen was an original thinker, something that often is a detriment in theology—and often with good warrant. He was born in Alexandria around 185 and spent much of his life there, becoming a philosopher and theologian. He is said to have written many hundreds of books,[7] almost none of which survive, perhaps

---

7 Origen's output may have exceeded even that of the prolific Barbara Cartland, a much later theologian.

because, after Origen's death, the emperor Justinian declared him a heretic and ordered all of his books to be burned.[8]

One of the few books of Origen's to survive in its entirety is *Against Celsus*. Celsus was a pagan philosopher known as the top opponent of Christianity in the ancient world and as the developer of a method to measure temperature.[9]

Origen is credited—or discredited, depending on one's point of view—with teaching the *apokatastasis*, the notion that at the end of time all creatures in hell, even Satan, will reconcile with God and enter heaven. He probably didn't teach this, but he ended up being identified with the *apokatastasis* anyway, such being the breaks of theological history.

Whatever Origen's views on such a final reconciliation, he held enough other questionable views that, although he was an early Christian writer, he never has been counted among the Fathers of the Church.

Multiple Claimants

The third century was a time of turmoil, particularly at the top of the ruling ladder. Roman emperors came and went. Mostly they went. In the 33 years from 251 to 284 there were eleven emperors. Not one of them

---

8 This may have been the only imperial order ever to be carried out punctiliously. Scholars wish the honor had gone elsewhere.

9 Eventually his method won out over that devised by a later pagan philosopher named Fahrenheit, except in America, which was named after Amerigo Vespucci, an Italian explorer who never even set foot in America. Go figure.

died in his own bed. About half died on the battlefield, and the others were murdered, either by the imperial troops who had elected them or by the troops of their political opponents. At one point there were nineteen rival claimants to the throne, all claiming to be The Real Emperor.

In the Middle Ages (more on this later) the best the Church could do was to have three rival papal claimants at one time. That was considered progress, as was the fact that in the Middle Ages nearly all popes died in their own beds.

The Roman emperors were a fickle lot. Some of them tolerated Christianity. Others persecuted it. Still others see-sawed between toleration and persecution. Diocletian is a good example. His wife and daughter were converts to Christianity, and he had many Christians working in his household, yet he started a fierce persecution in 303. It didn't end until his successor, Constantine, issued the Edict of Milan in 313.

Donatism

During Diocletian's persecution, not a few Christians cooperated with Roman authorities. When officials asked whether the Christians owned any religious books, they said yes and handed them over to the officials, who destroyed the books. This was more common in urban areas than in rural areas, where there was greater resistance to the persecution.

Some rural folk became resentful against those considered *traditores*, which means "those who hand over" holy things, and they began a movement called Donatism, which, in yet another wild coincidence, was named after a fellow, Donatus, who had been elected bishop of Carthage.

The Donatists flourished in North Africa and were rigorists. They claimed that priests who had been *traditores* could not celebrate sacraments validly because the Church consisted only of saints, not of sinners. This proved an attractive recruiting device for the Donatist sect, since many people wanted to associate only with others who were as faultless as they were.

The sect remained active for centuries, disappearing only once Islam overran North Africa. One of the opponents of Donatism, later in the fourth century, was Augustine, who lucked out and had the chance to write against many heresies.

Battle of the Milvian Bridge

Constantine became the emperor some years after Diocletian retired. He had a rival whose name was Maxentius. Their armies met for battle at the Milvian Bridge, which is located a couple of miles from Rome's Flaminian Gate.

The night before the battle Constantine had a dream in which he saw a large cross in the sky and heard a voice saying, *"In Hoc Signo Vinces"* ("In This Sign [the Cross] Conquer"), sometimes abbreviated as IHS. Those who have watched too many James Bond movies think "IHS" meant "In His [or Her Majesty's Secret] Service." Actually, "IHS" represents the first three letters of the name Jesus in Greek, so there is a double confusion.

However that may be, Constantine followed the dream's instructions, and his army won. He entered

Rome, convinced that the real God was the one that the Christians worshiped, thus proving that he was an astute man.

Constantine: Church Founder?

Modern Protestant Fundamentalists claim that it was Constantine who established the Catholic Church, through his legalization of Christianity. This is not true, as these people would know if they had read the earlier parts of this book. No more need be said.

Theodosius

Constantine, who reigned until 337, has been accused by modern writers of the Fundamentalist persuasion of making Christianity the state religion. This also was untrue. The fellow wasn't even baptized until he was on his deathbed.

Making Christianity the state religion was left to one of Constantine's successors, Emperor Theodosius, who reigned from 379 to 395 and who deserves proper credit.

He was a rare thing among Roman emperors: a believing, practicing Catholic. This is why, fifteen and sixteen centuries later, he never got A Good Press from secular historians. Besides, Theodosius didn't have a Milvian Bridge to crow about, so he was less interesting than Constantine to write about.[10]

---

10 Theodosius was the last man to rule the entire Roman world as sole emperor. You'd think this, at least, would have made him mentionable in modern history books, but it didn't, demonstrating that History Is Unfair.

Arius

Early in the fourth century there was a priest in Alexandria named Arius. He was a smart fellow who may have studied too much Greek philosophy. He probably also studied Eleutherius. He found himself unable to understand how Jesus could be at once God and Man. Arius concluded that Jesus was just a man, though the Best Man Ever.

This was called Doctrinal Simplification, and it proved to be very popular. Arius himself proved to be very popular—and a nuisance.

First Council of Nicaea

The first general (or ecumenical) council was called to deal with Arius's heretical teaching. It was held in 325 at Nicaea, in what is now Turkey.

Arius attended and spelled out his beliefs plainly. The bishops in attendance were not impressed. At length the council came up with a definitive definition that explained the relationship of God the Father and "Jesus Christ, the Son of God, the sole-begotten of the Father."

A minority of the bishops initially had wanted to use the term *homoiousios*, which means "of like substance," to explain the relationship, but the majority of the bishops settled on *homoousios*, which means "of the same substance." This meant that Jesus wasn't merely *like* God in his essence but actually *was* himself God.

The only difference between the two Greek terms was the letter iota, rendered in Latin characters as the letter *i*. Iota was the smallest Greek letter, but it was made even smaller in that in the word *homoiousios* the first *i* was written beneath the preceding vowel so scribes could save one letter space, which was a big deal before the invention of the Linotype. Putting the first iota beneath the preceding letter made that iota really small, as though it were of no importance.

The Arian party said, "Hey, what's the fuss? It doesn't make an iota of difference which term we choose, so choose ours." The Catholic party said, "Pound sand. We have the votes." In the end, all but two of the bishops signed off on the new definition, which then became definitively definitive.

Arianism Gets Imperial Help

That should have ended the matter, but it didn't. Arianism, as the heresy was known, took on a life of its own. Even many bishops and priests subscribed to it because it was easier to think of Christ as having one nature rather than two, inasmuch as everyone in everyone's neighborhood had only one nature.

Arianism lasted for centuries, and in practice, even if not with that title, it is held by many today. They believe that Jesus was the Best Man Ever, but that's it.

What kept Arianism going in the early years, well beyond the death of Arius, was its promotion by Roman emperors, to whom Arius's party had appealed. By this time the emperors had become used to sticking their noses into Church business, and the results usually were bad.

This fact could have been used by Thomas Jefferson to argue on behalf of the separation of church and state, but Jefferson belonged to no church at all, and so the thought never occurred to him.

Athanasius

To combat Arianism the Church had one of the greatest bishops of antiquity, Athanasius. He was elected bishop of Alexandria, the most important see in North Africa, and he soon went into battle against the Arians. There were so many of them that he was known as Athanasius Contra Mundum, or Athanasius Against the World.

He was the first and last man in history to be given that sobriquet, and just as well. You don't end up with many friends if you're Against the World.

Julian the Non-Apostate

All of the emperors who succeeded Constantine were Christians, at least nominally, except for one. He came to be known as Julian the Apostate, but this was a little unfair. He never had been a Christian, so he couldn't have apostatized from the Christian religion, but he did seek to bring back paganism. That worked for about two weeks.

Augustine

Augustine was the greatest theologian of antiquity. His mother was named Monica.

She is famous for having prayed unceasingly that he would straighten out his life and become a Christian. Eventually he did so, but only after his mother became thoroughly exasperated with him, which is distressingly common when mothers have sons.

Augustine ended up as bishop of the city of Hippo, which was located on the shore of the Mediterranean

in what is now Algeria. The city's name was a curious one, since the nearest known hippopotami were located along the upper Nile, nearly two thousand miles away.

Augustine is best known as the author of *The Confessions*. The book was a runaway best-seller, perhaps because the title suggested salacious content, but it contained nothing of the sort. Many ancient readers seem to have been disappointed, but they had no recourse. This was in the days before Amazon, when it was not possible to return books purchased under a misapprehension.

Augustine published his final book, *The City of God*, in 426. Four years later he died at Hippo, and three years after that Hippo was captured and destroyed by barbarians known as the Vandals because they engaged in vandalism, which had been a problem for centuries. Apparently the Vandals had become upset on discovering that *The Confessions* wasn't what they thought it to be.

Pelagianism

One heretic against whom Augustine wrote was Pelagius. The two men were born in the same year, 354. This was convenient, since otherwise 354 was a dull year, the only other historical events being a circus and theater shows hosted by the Emperor Constantius to mark the thirtieth year of his reign.

Reacting against Manichaeism, which held that spiritual things were made by God and were good while material things were made by A Bad Creator and were bad, Pelagius taught that everything created was good and therefore God could not have allowed men to have a fallen nature. They were free to do good or evil and could live perfect lives, if they so chose. Adam's sin didn't corrupt everyone's human nature. It only set a bad example, which could be ignored, the way we ignore bad examples set by bank robbers.

Pelagius's teaching was welcomed by those short of cash.

Martin of Tours

When Augustine and Pelagius were 43, there died a famous bishop, Martin of Tours. He was the first person who wasn't a martyr to be recognized as a saint. Before that, you weren't a saint unless you managed to get yourself killed, which was easy to do in the early centuries.

Much later Martin, who for a time had been a soldier and had gotten around quite a bit, became the patron saint of travelers, cruise lines, and tourist agencies, and that is how he got his title.

Nestorius

Nestorius became the patriarch of Constantinople in 428. He immediately caused a public stir by claiming that the Virgin Mary should be called "Christ Bearer" (*Christotokos*) but not "God Bearer" (*Theotokos*). Nestorius wanted to emphasize the distinction between Christ's divine nature and his human nature, but he overdid it.

People were not happy with him, and a general council was convened in 431 at Ephesus, in present-day Turkey, to determine which *Tokos* was the right one.

Nestorius lost the argument, lost his bishopric, and was exiled to a monastery in the Egyptian desert, where he died twenty years later. His theological ideas did not die with him, and several religious bodies in the East adopted some of his views, even to this day.

Council of Chalcedon

Although no one knew it at the time, Isaac Newton's principle of "equal and opposite reaction" came into play. As a response to Nestorianism—not exactly as a contradiction of its teachings but rather of the teachings of Arianism—there arose the heresy of Monophysitism, which held that in Christ there was only one nature (the divine) and not two (the divine and the human). This was the opposite of Arianism, which held that Christ had only a human nature.

Although Monophysites and Arians often came to blows with one another, they should not be considered enemies but competitors. Their underlying principle was the same: in Christ there could be only one nature. The thinking was that it was too hard to think how Christ could manage two natures, so he must have had only one, and it was just a question of choosing between the two.

The matter was decided by still another general council, this time held in 451 in Chalcedon, another town in present-day Turkey. (No one ever has explained the attraction of Turkey back then. There weren't even any Turks there yet.) The council decided that both disputants were wrong and that Christ indeed has two natures. The Monophysites and Arians also were told to pound sand.

Collapse of the Roman Empire

The Roman Empire collapsed officially, as distinguished from unofficially, in 476, when the last Roman emperor, a young fellow called Romulus Augustulus, was shoved off his throne by a barbarian general. The barbarians still seemed to have been upset with Augustine.

Romulus Augustulus disappeared into the dustbin of history, and so did the Roman Empire. It was dark in the dustbin, so the succeeding period was known as the Dark Ages. People forgot about *The Confessions* and no longer were upset with Augustine, so something good came of the affair.

Period 2

The Dark Ages

500 to 1000

Benedict

Benedict was born in Nursia, which is not far from Assisi (at least if one has access to a car, which Benedict didn't). He has become a patron saint of Europe, whereas Patrick (see next entry) has had to settle for a lesser place and merely gets an annual parade in New York.

Benedict was adept at founding monasteries — about a dozen of them in and around Subiaco, where he began his religious life by spending three years hiding out in a cave high on the side of a cliff. He also founded the abbey of Monte Cassino, where he died.[11]

Benedict was famous for writing a Rule, which is a set of regulations for monks. His Rule was popular because it wasn't as strict as the regulations governing monks who lived in the East, such as in Egypt.

Benedict's motto was *ora et labora*, which means "pray and work." This appealed to men who liked to

---

11 The abbey itself died in 1944, when the Allies bombed it to smithereens because the Germans had been holding out in it. The abbey was rebuilt a decade later, no doubt to Benedict's satisfaction.

pray, but not all the time, and who liked to work, but not all the time. It never appealed to men who liked neither to pray nor to work. Such men became politicians instead.

Patrick

In Britain—no one knows exactly when or where—a boy of sixteen named Patrick was captured in a raid by the Irish and sold into slavery. After six years of working as a shepherd, he managed to escape to Gaul, where he eventually became a bishop and was assigned to return to Ireland to preach the faith there.

Although there already were Catholics in Ireland, Patrick came to be known as the founder of Catholicism on that island. This was good, because he happened to have the most popular Irish name.[12]

Patrick was successful in reorganizing the Church in Ireland. He also helped Ireland materially, being said to have driven the snakes out of the country. Where he drove them is unknown, but there are six municipalities in the United States named after him, and each one is noted for a high incidence of reptiles. That may not be a coincidence.

Gregory the Great

While Benedict is known as the founder of Western monasticism, it was Pope Gregory the Great who is called the founder of the Middle Ages. He was born

---

12 There is no evidence at all that he ever was called Paddy. That would not have been sufficiently dignified for a bishop.

in Rome of an aristocratic family in 540, eight years before Benedict died. They never met.

It was Gregory who sent the first missionaries to Britain. Among them was Augustine, who was not the late bishop of Hippo but another man of the same name. This other Augustine became popular in Britain, but he was not the Augustine for whom the city of St. Augustine, Florida, was named, and just as well, since that city's residents never have learned how to pronounce the name of their city properly.

As for Gregory, he came from quite a good background. His father was a Roman senator. (That was an honorable position and is not to be confused with modern-day senators, of whatever country.) Gregory proved to be an accomplished leader. He cleaned up and reorganized many things in the Church. He was the first successful Church administrator. He also may have been the last.

However that may be, it is indisputable that he was an accomplished writer. He wrote more than all the preceding popes combined, but in fairness it needs to be acknowledged that most of them apparently wrote nothing at all.

Especially important were Gregory's writings and regulations regarding the Mass. Before his time, the Mass in the West existed in many variants. He revised the Mass, and by the Middle Ages he was known as "the Father of Christian Worship." He ended up being admired not just by Catholics but by Eastern Orthodox and even by Protestants. John Calvin declared that Gregory was the last good pope.[13]

---

13 It has not been established what Gregory would have considered Calvin to have been, but one can imagine.

Council of Toledo

After the fall of the Roman Empire, many peoples migrated from one part of Europe to another. The Visigoths were a Germanic tribe that headed west, first to Gaul, from which they were booted, and then to Hispania, which later became Spain.

The Visigoths of Spain were Arians, but that was fixed at the Council of Toledo in 589.

The Visigothic prince, Reccared, and his nobles were in attendance, as were 64 bishops. The prince and most of his entourage formally repudiated Arianism and subscribed to a profession of faith that included the Filioque Clause—the very thing that threw Eastern Christians into a snit three centuries later.

Carrying out the edicts of the council was left to Leander, the archbishop of Seville, who was a friend of Gregory the Great and who effected the conversion of Reccared to Catholicism. Leander died in 600 and was succeeded by his brother, Isidore of Seville, who, as already noted, is counted as the last Father of the Church in the West.

One result of the Council of Toledo was the burgeoning union of Church and state.[14] Loyalty to the Church became equated with patriotism, and anything non-Catholic became regarded as anti-Spanish. This attitude had its negative elements, but it gave Spanish Catholics cohesion when Spain was overrun by the Moors.[15]

---

14 Thomas Jefferson wasn't around to oppose it, but it likely would have proceeded despite his opposition.

15 But barely enough. As noted later, they lost almost all of Spain to the Moors, but "not all" is better than "all."

Monothelitism

First there was Arianism, which said Christ had only a human nature. Then there was Monophysitism, which said that he had only a divine nature. The long, sorry stories of these heresies should have ended the infatuation with the number one, but they didn't, theological hobby horses being difficult to dismount from.

In the seventh century there developed a new heresy, Monothelitism, which said Christ had but one will, the divine, and that he had no human will at all. The chief proponent of this theory was Sergius, the patriarch of Constantinople, but Sergius didn't act alone. He had secular help.

As had become commonplace, the Byzantine emperor—Heraclius, in this case—intruded into the affray, emperors having become persistent ecclesiastical busybodies. Heraclius saw Monothelitism as a way to undermine the Monophysitism that still persisted in some parts of his empire. He would play one theological speculation against the other, in order to unite his empire. Of course, it didn't work.[16]

On his part, Sergius wrote to Pope Honorius, asking him to affirm a theological argument that underlay the Monothelite position. Honorius replied with an ambiguous letter, saying the parties should calm down and stifle the argumentation. That was not helpful, and it ended up making Honorius look incompetent, mostly because he was.

What's more, it ended up getting Honorius condemned, though posthumously, at the Third Council

---

16 As he lay dying in 640, Heraclius, ever generous, placed all the blame for Monothelitism on Sergius.

of Constantinople, which opened in 680 and had as its focus the condemnation of Monothelitism. The council and its condemnations wouldn't be official until the pope, Leo II, confirmed them. He confirmed the condemnation of the heresy, but he interpreted the council as condemning Honorius not for teaching error but for "imprudent economy of silence"—in other words, for not speaking up when he should have.

Ever since, Honorius has been Exhibit No. 1 for those arguing against papal infallibility, even though Honorius never claimed to be deciding anything infallibly.[17] Such are the breaks of ill-intentioned argumentation.

Synod of Whitby

Britain, being on the periphery of Europe, was late in being evangelized. This was true particularly for what later became Scotland. Much of the evangelizing was done by monks from the western island of Iona and the eastern island of Lindisfarne, which became centers of Celtic Christianity.

Over time a controversy arose about Easter. The Celtic churches hadn't kept up with the times, particularly the times in Rome, which over the years had settled on a different way to calculate when Easter should be observed.

Monks argued against monks (something not at all uncommon), and eventually a synod was held at Whitby in 664. The Celtic bishop Colman claimed his

---

17 Popes aren't infallible when they deliberately decide not to decide. For some people, this is too subtle to comprehend.

people followed a liturgical calendar reaching back to the apostle John. He thought that would end the discussion. It didn't.

Wilfrid, a monk who formerly had lived at Lindisfarne but who had studied in Rome, championed the Roman usage. He pointed out that it was in Rome that Peter and Paul lived and died, and that should count for more than a tradition doubtfully stemming from John.

The issue was decided by the local prince, Oswy, who said that when he died and approached the gates to heaven, it would be Peter who would be there, not John, and Oswy didn't want to annoy the fellow with the keys, so he ordered the monks to adopt the Roman calendar. Disgusted, Colman left the synod. Some Celtic missionaries followed him, while others conformed. Those on the losing side are said to have taken up the bagpipe in order to annoy those on the winning side.

Spain and the Reconquista

In 711 a Moorish army crossed from North Africa to Gibraltar, invading Spain. On their way to Córdoba, the Moors routed the Spanish army, and they kept routing Spaniards they met until they ruled almost all of Spain. The Spaniards were left only with the tiny, mountainous area of Asturias at the extreme northern end of the Iberian Peninsula.

The Spaniards made a last stand under the leadership of Pelayo and prevailed at the battle of the Cave of Covadonga. The Moors, having taken control of everything else in Spain, decided it was time for a well-deserved siesta and thought they could ignore the Spanish remnant hiding among the crags. It was a capital mistake.

It was in Asturias that the Spaniards were able to consolidate their operations, and little by little, over the next seven centuries, they retook their land from the Moors in what was called the Reconquista. The last Moorish army was defeated in 1492, one reason Columbus felt free to sail westward.[18]

The Reconquista was the longest war in world history, and at the end of it everyone was exhausted. Islam had been eliminated from Spain after much hardship, but the ever-astute Spaniards preserved much Islamic architecture, repurposing mosques as churches, to the chagrin of Muslims, who did the reverse in Constantinople and elsewhere in the East.[19]

The victorious Spanish armies were much praised throughout Europe, other parts of which were having problems with Muslim invaders, and Spanish knights were held in high esteem. One of the best known was a man from La Mancha, a fellow named Quixote, who wrote a book with the help of a ghost writer named Cervantes.

Battle of Tours

In eighth-century Gaul, which a while later would be called France, there were incursions from Saracen-held Spain. The Saracens not long before had been called Moors, and the Christian soldiers they fought were

18 Aside from the situation with Alexander VI, which will be explained later.

19 Both sides believed that "turnabout is fair play," which often it isn't.

called, for some reason, Franks rather than Gaullists.[20] It was a confusing time in terms of nomenclature.

The leader of the Franks was Charles Martel. He is remembered for leading an army that defeated Saracen forces at Tours[21] in 732, his infantry routing their cavalry. This proved to be the furthest incursion made by Muslim forces into the Christian West.

Charles Martel was succeeded by Pepin the Short, who in turn was succeeded by Charlemagne, who was notably taller than Pepin but who, out of respect for his predecessor, never was called Charles the Tall. He preferred being called Charles the Great anyway, and who wouldn't have?

Siege of Constantinople

The Eastern counterpart to the battle of Tours was the siege of Constantinople. That began in 717, when an army of eighty thousand Saracens and a fleet of one thousand ships appeared before the Christian capital.

The Christians' leader was a future heretic, the Emperor Leo III. He had spent months shoring up Constantinople's defenses, and everyone was surprised when it turned out that the defenders had more food supplies than did the attackers, who had expected to overrun the capital quickly but who instead ended up getting hungry slowly.

At a propitious moment, Leo's ships were sent out among the Saracen ships and employed "Greek fire," the forerunner to the modern flame-thrower, and

20 This reserved *Gaullists* as a name for a future French political movement, so everything worked out okay.

21 This town hosted more than its fair share of events and personages, an example of history playing favorites.

ended up burning most of the Saracen ships. Saracen sailors were not amused. Nor were Saracen soldiers, a quarter of whom eventually fell to the Byzantine army. The Saracens went home after having had A Bad Time, but after the East was secured for Christians, it was the Christians' turn to have A Bad Time as Leo turned from warfare to Iconoclasm.

Iconoclasm

In 787 Nicaea found itself hosting another general council of the Church. This council was called to settle a controversy that had been plaguing the East for several decades: whether images and relics of saints should be venerated and whether prayers to saints were lawful.

Six emperors had been dethroned in the space of 21 years, but Leo III took the throne in Constantinople in 717 and sat on it for 23 years.[22] For reasons historians never have understood, when the Iconoclastic heresy arose around 725, Leo became its leading patron. Over the next five years he issued several decrees against the veneration of images.

The public was split. Those who lived in the east-ernmost parts of the Empire, where Muslims made frequent and harrowing incursions, tended to sup-port Iconoclasm, because they had been influenced by Muslim thinking.

On the other hand, citizens of the Byzantine Empire who lived in Constantinople, the Balkan areas, and the provinces in Italy tended to oppose Iconoclasm. They liked paintings, mosaics, and statues and didn't make an error that still is made by not a few non-Catholics

---

22 To be clear: he got up from the throne as necessary.

today: they didn't assume that someone kneeling before, praying before, or lighting a candle before an image must be worshiping that image as though it were itself divine. But Leo made that assumption, to the general discombobulation of his subjects.

He began to persecute those who venerated images. He did this until the end of his reign, when he was succeeded by his son, Constantine V, who doubled down on his father's efforts.

The new emperor wrote a treatise in which he said that images of Christ must be destroyed because they depicted him as a man and thus implied that he had a human nature only. This was silly thinking, but one must remember that, like his father, Constantine was a politician, and politicians are not noted for nuance.

Orthodox-leaning bishops called a council. It was held at Nicaea. The pope did not attend, but he sent legates with a letter approving the veneration of images, and the council fathers replied, "We follow, we receive, we admit," which was a roundabout way of saying "Yes."

After the council, artists saw a boom in business, and rightly so.

Charlemagne

Charlemagne, who had been king of the Franks for quite some time, was crowned Holy Roman Emperor by Pope Leo III on Christmas Day, 800. That year was chosen because it was a nice, round number that people thought would be auspicious. It turned out they were right. The Holy Roman Empire lasted until 1806 (1,006 years in all), which was twice as long as the original

HOLY
ROMAN
EMPIRE
800
1806

Roman Empire lasted, at least in the West, and therefore the Holy Roman Empire was twice as good as the original. The Emperor Augustus might not have been happy with the comparison, but the empire he founded had a fine run, so he earns high marks regardless.

More remarkable, the Holy Roman Empire lasted more than eighty times as long as a twentieth-century empire that was supposed to last for a thousand years but that fizzled out after only twelve, proving that the Holy Roman Empire was more than eighty times as good as the modern attempt, which sounds about right.

Eastern Complaints

Half a century later, things were in an uproar in Constantinople. The patriarch had died, and his successor, Ignatius, wanted to cleanse God's house. After ten years of trying to do so—not with much success—he came into conflict with the court, which intrigued to have him deposed.

The effort was led by an archbishop called Gregory Asbestas, who was said to have a hot temper. He had been deposed by Ignatius and carried a grudge.

As grudges tend to do historically, this grudge had long-lasting consequences. The emperor was a teenager, and it was his regent who really ran things. Ignatius and the regent, who was egged on by Gregory Asbestas, had a spat, with the result that Ignatius was arrested and banished. In his place as patriarch was put Photius.

Photius and his supporters appealed to Pope Nicholas I, seeking approval of the new arrangement.

They invented a tale about how Ignatius voluntarily had resigned. The pope, after listening to them, sent his own men to investigate the situation. They returned to Rome and informed the pope that Ignatius was the rightful patriarch and that Photius was a usurper. The pope said Ignatius should be reinstated.

Luckily for himself, Photius had the imperial court on his side. He refused to accept Rome's decisions and struck the pope's name out of the Mass. Nicholas sent a long letter in reply.

He reminded Photius that the papacy was of divine origin and, by implication, that Photius's position wasn't. Arguments went back and forth for a few years, and then Photius sent an encyclical letter to the other bishops in the East, listing his complaints with the Church of the West.

He didn't like it that the Westerners fasted on Saturday, looked down on married priests, and ate milk-based foods during the three days before Ash Wednesday. This last complaint meant that Photius rejected Mardi Gras (Fat Tuesday), but, admittedly, he had not yet had a chance to visit New Orleans.

The Filioque Clause

Photius's most long-lasting complaint was about the Filioque Clause. He said Westerners had corrupted the Creed by adding "and the Son" to the clause that says the Holy Spirit "proceeds from the Father." This was a good talking point in terms of local politics, but it wasn't a good talking point in terms of theology.

If the Son proceeds only from the Father, and if the Holy Spirit proceeds only from the Father (rather than from the Father and the Son), then the Son and the Holy Spirit would seem to have the same procession and would be duplicative, reducing the Trinity to a Duo.

The rupture instigated by Photius bubbled and simmered for nearly a century and a half before finally resulting in the East breaking off from the West in a definitively definitive way, but more on that shortly.

Skipping a Century

The tenth century was an unhappy one in Rome. It marked the historical low point for the Church, in terms of the morality and sensibility of its leadership, particularly at the top. It was A Bad Time. The less said the better.

Period 3

The Middle Ages

1000 to 1500

1054: Year of Disaster

If the tenth century featured a string of sorry men at the top in Rome, the eleventh century featured a schism that has persisted now for a millennium. The proximate cause was Michael Cerularius. He came from a senatorial family and worked his way up the ranks of the Byzantine Empire. He was appointed patriarch of Constantinople in 1043.

In the years leading up to that, several weak men succeeded one another on the papal throne in Rome. Cerularius took note.

A good pope, Leo IX, was elected in 1049, but Cerularius particularly disliked him because Leo was German, and Cerularius held Germans in low esteem. He thought Leo would be a pushover. He wasn't. (Germans seldom are.)

In 1052 Cerularius thought he saw his chance and closed the Latin churches in Constantinople. The next year he maneuvered a local bishop into denouncing Latin customs, including the use of unleavened bread in the Eucharist. Then a monk denounced clerical celibacy, something Pope Leo had been trying to bolster.

All this prompted a letter from Leo to Cerularius. The pope said "all false doctrines and heresies have been combated and condemned by the see of Rome" whereas the occupants of the see of Constantinople had included Arians, Nestorius himself, a Monophysite, Monothelites, and other heretics. Cerularius's reply to Leo has been lost, but apparently he wanted to make a deal in which he would become "the pope of the East."

The pope's answer was delivered by three legates. They arrived in Constantinople in March 1054. They hung around for months, making little progress with the patriarch. Finally, exasperated and seeing that he intended to persist in schism, on July 16 they entered Hagia Sophia, which was jam packed because a liturgy was about to begin, and placed a bull of excommunication on the altar. Then they went home.

Pope Leo didn't know about the bull because he had died three months earlier. In those days, international communication was slow, Alexander Graham Bell not having been born yet. It is not known whether Leo would have approved of the bull, but he had given his legates the authority to issue one, if necessary.

The excommunication of Cerularius marked the culmination of the split between the East and the West, making 1054 a fateful year. From this sad affair we have the ditty "East is East and West is West and never the twain shall meet," which was coined by a medieval writer named Kipling.

Berengarius

By this time the Church had existed for more than a thousand years, and in all those years no one ever had doubted, at least in print, the teaching of the Real Presence of Christ in the Eucharist. This ended with Berengarius of Tours (no relation to Martin of Tours), who claimed that, after the Consecration, Christ really was present, but so were regular bread and wine and not just the appearances of bread and wine.

Berengarius was a philosopher rather than a theologian. Like not a few philosophers early in the history of the Church (and since), he let his logical skills lead him to illogical ends—and to trouble with Church authorities. In the same year that the final split between the East and the West occurred, 1054, Berengarius laid out his thinking at a council held in France at Sens, and the bishops there decided he was senseless.

The Lay Investiture Controversy

As Europe moved toward the Middle Ages, lots of petty lords reigned over petty kingdoms. Some of these lords were bishops who ran their dioceses like regular princedoms. When a secular lord died, his son inherited his domain. But what happened when a bishop died? There being no son (one hoped), the domain (diocese) went to the local secular lord, who then began lording it over the Church. Such lords took it upon themselves to name successor bishops, figuring that the local Church was their property to manage as they pleased.

So began the lay investiture controversy. At the highest level, for many years the Holy Roman emperors decided which men would become popes. Romans of all sorts grew tired of this, and in 1057 the Roman clergy elected a man of their own choosing, informing the emperor of the new pope only after the pope had been on the job a while.

A few years later there was another pope, Nicholas II, best remembered as the pope who wrote the law governing papal elections. With modest changes, his law has persisted down to our own time, which is more than can be said for most any laws.

Gregory VII

There followed, for more than a decade, efforts to reform the administration of the Church. Eventually there was enough interest in doing so that a brilliant adviser to several popes, Hildebrand, was elected to the papacy. He took the name Gregory VII. He issued decrees against simony and clerical concubinage, but these and other reform efforts didn't get far because corrupt bishops and priests liked being corrupt. The only way around that, thought Gregory, was to get rid of lay investiture, which he did. Or at least he started to do so, since the effort took many years.

Gregory VII is remembered for his encounter with the Holy Roman Emperor Henry IV at Canossa in 1077. Henry had been booted out of the Church and came to Canossa dressed as a simple penitent. He stood in the snow, in front of the castle gates, for three days, asking the pope's pardon. The pope suspected the emperor wasn't sincere (after all, Henry was a politician), but he had little choice but to absolve him anyway.

Call to the Crusades

Two decades later, in 1095, the pope was Urban II, so called because he preferred city life over rural life. It

had come to his attention, as it also had come to the attention of his predecessors over the prior several centuries, that Christians in the Holy Land in particular and in the East in general were being persecuted by Muslims who had conquered what once had been Christian lands, such as the Holy Land in particular and the East in general.

In November there assembled a large council in Auvergne, a region in central France. There were 264 bishops, more than four hundred abbots, thousands of lesser clergy, and, it was said, more than one hundred thousand lay folk who gathered to make sure the Churchmen actually accomplished something.

On November 27 Urban made his famous speech. It was so famous that no record of his words survives, but it was an appeal to the vast throng before him to save the Christians of the Holy Land in particular and of the East in general from the depredations of the Muslims. Urban seems to have been a good orator: the entire crowd yelled "God wills it!" Many knights, nobles, and not-so-nobles vowed to take up their swords. Their symbol was to be a cross cut from red cloth, and from this came the name *crusader*[23] for those who participated.

In the following centuries there were several distinct crusades, a few of them at least temporarily successful but most not. In the long run the Holy Land in particular and the East in general remained in the hands of Muslims.

---

23 The word *crusader* maintained its positive aura for centuries. The Author recalls that the sports teams at his public junior high school were called "the Crusaders," but this was before modern sensibilities intruded and spoiled the fun.

Concordat of Worms

The investiture controversy continued into the next century. It reached a resolution at the Concordat of Worms, which many still mistakenly believe had something to do with invertebrates used in fishing. Actually, Worms was a German city that, for reasons obscure to historians, got stuck with an awkward name. The Concordat was an agreement, signed in 1122, between the papacy and the Holy Roman Empire regarding the appointment of bishops and abbots.

The emperor, Henry V, renounced his right to invest ecclesiastics with the ring and crosier, the symbols of their ecclesiastical authority, while the pope, Callixtus II, said the emperor could invest them with the scepter, the symbol of the civil authority such clerics commonly held.

It was a simple solution to a problem that had plagued the Church for decades. Everyone went away happy, the pope and emperor heading off together to Worms' bait shop.

Lateran I

The fishing having gone well at Worms, the next year the pope convened the first general council to be held in the West. It was held at his own cathedral church in Rome, the Basilica of St. John Lateran.

There the assembled bishops—more than five hundred of them—confirmed the agreements made at Worms and, most significantly, decided that any man who was ordained a priest could not enter into a valid marriage. This began to eliminate the problem of priests having concubines.

The council bishops thought this was fine, since, from the earliest centuries, bishops had to be chosen from, and had to remain, unmarried men, meaning the new canon didn't affect them. It did affect others. It is said that not a few men who otherwise had been considering holy orders opted to become accountants instead, and just as well.

Bernard of Clairvaux

The most impressive man of the first half of the twelfth century was Bernard, the abbot of Clairvaux. He was the dominant intellectual of his time, and it is said that nothing of consequence happened in the Church without his active intervention.

More importantly, he was the dominant spiritual figure of his time, known for extraordinary asceticism and for eloquence not seen since the time of Ambrose, who had taught Augustine (not the Augustine in England but the one mispronounced in Florida).

Dante was so impressed by Bernard that the poet made the great saint his guide, in *The Divine Comedy*, through the upper stages of heaven. (There is no indication that Beatrice, who had been Dante's guide in heaven's earlier stages, felt miffed.)

Lateran II

In 1139 the Second Lateran Council was held. It dealt with a theme popular in our own time, social justice. The council passed several decrees.

The first decree ordered a halt to the long-standing custom in which, after a bishop died, the people of the diocese were permitted to pillage his house. This decree was greeted warmly by relations of bishops within the third degree.

Another decree ordered a stop to usury, to which a stop had been ordered before, with about as little success as this decree proved to have.

A third decree ordered that the Truce of God would apply throughout Christendom. It had begun a century and a half before, and the council fathers thought it time to make it universal.

The Truce of God was an attempt to limit warfare, which was endemic in feudal times. Seasons and days were put off limits, the knights errant and errant knights having to stand down and cool off. Gradually more and more seasons and days were added to the list, until warfare was permitted only on alternate Thursday afternoons outside of Lent.

Going further to stick it to the knights, the council decreed that knights who were killed in jousts were not to be given Christian burial. Everyone except joust organizers and undertakers applauded this advance.

Lastly, the catapult, capable of hurtling large masses of stone at the walls of castles and cities, was condemned as "detested by God" because the catapult was a weapon of mass destruction. Those who used catapults were to be excommunicated.

As an unforeseen consequence of this ruling, the cannon was invented.

Thomas Becket

In England, the archbishop of Canterbury, Theobald of Bec, was looking for an assistant and chose a young man who may have been a distant relative, Thomas

Becket. Becket proved to be so effective that Theobald recommended him to the king, Henry II, to be lord chancellor, which Becket became in 1155.

Becket and the king got on famously, until they didn't.

After Theobald died, Becket was made archbishop of Canterbury. Henry expected that Becket would continue to put the king's interests above the Church's interests. Henry expected wrongly.

Becket resigned as lord chancellor and began to try to regain rights that once had belonged to the archbishopric. This displeased Henry, and Becket went into exile in France. Later, Henry went to France, and Becket went to England. This was in 1170.

While Becket was in Canterbury, he further annoyed the king, who famously asked, "Will no one rid me of this turbulent priest?" Except that's not what Henry actually said.

He actually said, "What miserable drones and traitors have I nourished and brought up in my household, who let their lord be treated with such shameful contempt by a low-born cleric?"

That proved not to be memorable, so Henry's quotation was altered in 1740 by an unknown person adept at the Art of Public Relations. Thereafter, Henry became known as worthy of being quoted, even if only centuries after his death.

Whatever the king actually said, it was enough to induce four of his knights to travel to England and murder Becket. The murder occurred in the sanctuary of Canterbury's cathedral, which is why T. S. Eliot named his 1935 play *Murder in the Cathedral*. What else could he have named it?

Peter Waldo

In the second half of the twelfth century a rather troublesome figure came into prominence. He was a wealthy banker who lived in Lyons, and his name was Peter Waldo.

He came upon the biblical admonition "If you will be perfect, sell all you have" (Matt. 19:21), and he did so, giving half to his wife and half to the poor, keeping nothing for himself.

Waldo became a self-appointed preacher, something that seldom ends well, as the whole history of Protestantism shows.

Waldo proved to be a good speaker and soon had a large following. He went from town to town, and the common people looked forward to his arrival, asking one another, "Where's Waldo?" They made a game of it, and the game has persisted to this day.

Waldo and his followers, known as Waldenses, soon claimed that those not mimicking their lives of poverty weren't good Catholics.

This didn't sit well with the archbishop of Lyons, who was a Catholic, or with the pope, who also was a Catholic. The archbishop and the pope told Waldo and his followers to stop preaching. They replied, "We must follow God instead of men."

Soon the Waldenses were allowing women to preach[24] and saying that good works and Masses for the dead were useless. They claimed that bad priests

---

24 This may have inspired Samuel Johnson to say to James Boswell, centuries later, "Sir, a woman's preaching is like a dog's walking on his hind legs. It is not done well; but you are surprised to find it done at all." Then again, maybe not.

didn't have to be obeyed. This did not sit well with good priests, let alone bad ones, but Waldo and the Waldenses continued their itinerant activity.

Albigensianism

As troublesome as Waldo and the Waldenses were, they were sweetness and light compared to the Albigenses, who were their contemporaries.

The former became influential because they opposed laxity in the Church, which they wanted to reform. The latter became even more influential because they wanted to overthrow the Church, which they hated.

Albigensianism—named for the French town of Albi, where the movement flourished in the twelfth and thirteenth centuries—was a revival of ancient Manichaeism. Instead of believing in one God, the Albigenses taught there were two gods, one entirely good and the other entirely evil. Everything material was evil; only the spiritual was good.

In Albigensian eyes, Christ was neither God nor man but an angel, and his death was an illusion. The Catholic Church wasn't Christ's church, since the Catholic Church taught that Christ had been a true man, had died, and had risen again.

Multiple councils were called to condemn these teachings: Toulouse in 1119, Lateran II in 1139, Rheims in 1148, Tours in 1163, Lateran III in 1179. They failed to stem the advance of the heresy, which spread widely in France and Spain. Something had to be done.

That something was a man named Dominic. More on him shortly.

The Inquisition

In the Church's earliest centuries—at least after the Roman emperors had become Christians—heresy was considered to have two aspects, spiritual and political. Heresy was more than just erroneous religious opinion. It had an effect on civil life as well.

Heresy bothered the emperors (at least the ones who themselves weren't heretics) because it meant civil commotion, and they already had more than enough civil commotion to deal with.

What followed were attempts by civil authorities, then and in later times, to restrain heretics, many of whom spent their time fomenting and leading mobs. Mobs were Not Approved, but they happened anyway. Most of these attempts to restrain heretics and heresies were haphazard and unavailing. The Church professionalized things in the Medieval Inquisition, which actually proved a boon, or at least a salve, for the heretics themselves. They ended up getting better treatment in Church courts than in civil courts.

Civil authorities had been treating heretics rather roughly. King Robert II of France, for example, burned them at the stake, and King Henry II of England had them branded on the forehead. Not infrequently, these punishments were applied to people who, as it turned out, weren't really guilty.

Pope Alexander III disapproved, saying, "It is better to absolve the guilty than to attack innocent life by an excessive severity." This was in the twelfth century. Later, at Lateran IV in 1215, rules were set out regarding how heretics were to be handled. For example, it was declared that no one should be convicted of heresy except on the testimony of at least two witnesses.

Nearly six centuries later, the American Framers put a similar provision into the Constitution, saying no one should be convicted of treason except on the testimony of at least two witnesses, proving that the Church was ahead of the times.

Lateran IV

In 1215 the pope was Innocent III, so called because he never had much of interest to report when going to confession. It was he who convened the Fourth Lateran Council, the greatest of the Middle Ages. The council opened on November 11, which was Armistice Day, but not yet. There were 412 bishops, eight hundred abbots and priors, and many heads of religious orders. They worked quickly. They met in just three sessions, finishing on November 30. This marked the Church's apogee for episcopal efficiency.

Over the following centuries conciliar progress progressively slowed, until finally it took Vatican II four years to do its work, thus putting the lie to the modern claim that the Middle Ages were centuries of indolence.

The first canon was Lateran IV's most famous. It was a profession of faith and a clear rebuke to the Albigenses. It included the first official use of the word *transubstantiation*, but this was not the first time transubstantiation was believed.[25]

The second canon condemned a book written by an already-dead theologian, Joachim of Flora, an early

---

25 The first time was on Maundy Thursday, when Christ said, "This is my body," making the apostles the first believers in transubstantiation, even though that word hadn't been invented yet.

precursor of the New Age Movement. Joachim had posited three ages of Church history. The Age of the Father corresponded to Old Testament times. The Age of the Son was the time of the Church and would last until 1260 (just a few years away). The Age of the Holy Spirit would follow until the end of time and would be a utopian period in which the ecclesiastical order would be replaced by the Christian equivalent of the Age of Aquarius.

Other canons of Lateran IV set out punishments for errant clerics, much to their dismay but to the general approval of the Catholic faithful. Among other things, clerics were forbidden not only to participate in games of chance but even to observe them. Lay gamblers liked this provision because it increased their own odds.

Dominic

Dominic de Guzman was a Spaniard. He had observed how ineffective efforts had been to curb Albigenses, and in 1215 he decided a new religious order was needed, one consisting of preachers who would go around preaching against the heresy.

He named this order of preachers the Order of Preachers. It wasn't a catchy name, and so, in another wild coincidence, everyone ended up calling its members the Dominicans.

Dominic wanted his preachers to be the best anywhere, and he thought great preaching would come only from extensive studies in theology and philosophy. He placed stress on intellectual preparation, and the Dominicans became known as the Smart Guys of the Church, mostly because they were.

After rigorous training, Dominic's preachers went out and dominated public debates. Gradually they won over the well-educated and the uneducated. (The former often were the harder to convince, since they thought they already knew everything.) Eventually, Albigensianism subsided, largely due to the work of Dominic's men.

Oddly, even today many Catholics think Dominic invented the rosary. This is not true. The rosary existed long before his time. He invented clever promotion of the rosary, which was just about as important, because a devotion doesn't accomplish much if no one is devoted to it.

Francis of Assisi

Francis of Assisi was eleven years younger than Dominic. He was called "of Assisi" because he was born in Assisi, Italy. His father was in France on a business trip when Francis was born, and by his mother the boy was named Giovanni, but his father changed the name to Francis as soon as he got home because he had enjoyed his trip to France. There is no evidence that this caused the infant any Cognitive Dissonance.

Francis grew up in a wealthy household and lived a life common to the young men of his class. When he was around twenty-five, he prayed in the half-ruined church of San Damiano and was startled to hear a voice telling him to rebuild it, which he did. He didn't realize that God meant him to rebuild not just that church but the Church at large.

Later Francis heard the voice again and became an itinerant and dirt-poor preacher. He gathered like-minded men around him, and they had a great effect wherever they went, particularly on those who had been attracted to the Waldenses' lives of poverty. Within ten years there were five thousand Friars Minor (the second term not meaning that they were under voting age).

Francis died in 1226. Two years prior, while on a forty-day fast, he received the stigmata. He was the first person known to have received the marks of the Lord's Passion on his own body. A year before that, Francis visited Subiaco, where Benedict had lived so many centuries earlier, and there a fresco of Francis was painted. It still can be seen in a lower chapel, behind a Plexiglas screen that was put in place a little while after Francis's visit.

Frederick II

When Innocent III died in 1216, Frederick II, the future Holy Roman emperor, was 22 years old. He was determined, crafty, and entirely without scruples. He would become, at least in Europe, the Church's greatest foe during the thirteenth century.

That was the time of crusades. Seven times in ten years Frederick promised the pope who succeeded Innocent that he would lead a crusader army to the Holy Land in particular and to the East in general. Each time he reneged. He preferred to stay at home, polishing his plans for universal, or at least European, rule.

Finally, Frederick did prepare to embark with an army, but he dilly-dallied so long that pestilence broke out in his army's encampment, and many soldiers died. Frederick declared that he too had come down sick, but few believed him. His army dissolved, the remaining men went home, and Frederick went back to his scheming.

Years later Frederick actually did go to the Holy Land in particular and the East in general and, arriving in Jerusalem, crowned himself king there. He proved so unwelcome to the Christians of Jerusalem that, when he made his way to the ship that would take him back to Italy, the local butchers pelted him with offal.

For decades Frederick opposed, and sometimes literally fought, the popes. In 1245, at the Council of Lyons, the bishops put Frederick on trial and declared him deposed. In response, Frederick anticipatorily quoted Queen Victoria, saying he was "not amused." Five years later Frederick was dead, which amused nearly everyone else.

Thomas Aquinas

The thirteenth century was a time of political turmoil and intrigue, but it also was a time of great intellectual consolidation and advance. The most consolidated and advanced of all the writers of that era was Thomas Aquinas.

He was born in 1225 in the castle at Roccasecca, where his father served as Count of Aquino. When he was twenty, Thomas was sent to Paris to study under Albert the Great, who at the time was the Smartest Man in Europe. Thomas eventually would rise to that distinction himself.

Albert lived to be eighty. Thomas never reached fifty, yet the younger man produced a wide array of works that are read with profit to this very day. He wrote many commentaries, not just on Scripture but on the writings of earlier theologians and even on Aristotle, but he is most famous for the *Summa Contra Gentiles* and the *Summa Theologiae*.

These multi-volume works were intended for what Thomas called "beginners" in theology. Beginners in the thirteenth century apparently were more intelligent than graduate students in the twenty-first. (This often is cited as proof of the debilitations of modern education.)

However that may be, Thomas has come to be considered not just the Smartest Man in the Europe of his time but the Greatest Theologian of All Time, despite the fact that, when he was in school, his classmates called him "The Dumb Ox," a nickname taken from the title of a book by G. K. Chesterton.

Celestine V

For two years, beginning in 1292, the papal see was vacant. Half the papal electors were Frenchmen, and they didn't want an Italian pope. Half were Italians, and they didn't want a French pope. Since it took a two-thirds vote to elect a pope, there was no pope.

This annoyed common Christians—and no one more than an elderly hermit named Pietro da Morrone. He wrote to the cardinals, saying that keeping the Throne of Peter vacant was a scandal and insisting that they elect a new pope at once.

The cardinals wrote back to Pietro and said, "Okay, we elect you." This was not what Pietro had anticipated, but he went to Rome anyway and accepted the job, taking the name Celestine V. The new pope was a kindly fellow but entirely inexperienced as a leader of men, let alone as the leader of something as large as the Church. He soon realized that he wasn't cut out for the papacy, and he resigned after being pope for only five months.

His successor, Boniface VIII, was so fond of Celestine that he put the old man under house arrest, where he died in 1296. For his part, Dante, writing a quarter of a century later, was so fond of Boniface that in *The Divine Comedy* he put Boniface in hell.

No one now remembers Boniface, except for how Dante treated him, but such are the breaks of Great Literature.

Dante

Dante Alighieri was an epic poet who wrote an epic poem. He was born in Florence in 1265, died in Ravenna in 1321, and sent many people to hell, particularly his fellow Florentines (some of whom had arranged for him to be sent into exile, never to return) and a few popes, including Celestine V, who actually ended up being canonized after Dante's death, proving that Dante wasn't always as prescient as has been assumed.

Nevertheless, Dante was the Greatest Poet of All Time, with the possible exception of Ogden Nash. Those who may disagree with this characterization of Dante's talents risk ending up where Celestine V didn't, and deservedly so.

Dante's locational mistake regarding Celestine can be found in the *Inferno*, the first canticle of *The Divine Comedy*, which wasn't a comedy because there was

nothing funny about sending people to hell, even if by mistake. Dante made up for his faux pas in *Purgatorio* and *Paradiso*, where he placed several Florentines and popes who maybe shouldn't have been placed so high, so things balanced out.

Popes in Avignon

For centuries it had been customary, as it is customary even today, for popes to leave Rome during August and to head for a more salubrious climate, such as at Castel Gandolfo in the Alban Hills, where the heat and humidity weren't as oppressive as in Rome and the accommodations were Five Star.

Residents of Rome, if they could do likewise, did likewise. Unlike popes, they didn't end up at Five Star accommodations, but anything was better than Rome in August. With the onset of nicer weather, the popes and the people of Rome returned to the Eternal City, except for one memorable exception.

From 1309 to 1376 the popes hung out at Avignon, barely ever stepping out of that French city, not so much because they didn't want to as because they were under the thumb of French monarchs, who happened to live there. (Sometimes, though, the Avignon popes managed to sneak out of town to visit nearby Châteauneuf-du-Pape, a hilltop town famous for its wine.[26])

Altogether, seven popes resided in Avignon over a span of 67 years. This protracted period was called the Avignon Papacy by those who didn't object to it

---

26 Châteauneuf-du-Pape wine still is produced, and the Author recommends it highly. [End of commercial message.]

and The Babylonian Captivity of the Papacy by those who did.

One of those who did object was Catherine of Siena, who nagged Gregory XI until he returned the papal court to Rome. He died there a short time later, not from being nagged by a saint nor from the heat and humidity of August (he died in March) but from Causes Unknown, which until modern times were what killed most of the popes.

Great Western Schism

Instead of things improving, they got worse after Gregory XI's death. What followed his death was his funeral, and what followed his funeral was known as the Great Western Schism.

The Roman people didn't want the papacy to return to Avignon, so they pressured the cardinals to elect a local fellow, which they did. He took the name Urban VI.[27] He turned out to have a rather unpleasant personality, being pushy and argumentative, and the cardinals soon regretted their decision.

Five months later the cardinals met outside of Rome and elected another man as pope, Clement VII. The cardinals said their election of Urban had been invalid because they had been intimidated by the Roman populace.

This threw everything into confusion. In the past there had been anti-popes, but they had been elected by rival factions. Here it was the one and only faction that elected two different men, each of whom now

---

27 Like his predecessors of that name, he preferred to live in big cities rather than in small towns.

claimed to be the legitimate pope. (Years later, every-one acknowledged that the first election had been valid and that Urban VI, as unpleasant as he was, was the real pope, but this acknowledgment was yet a long way off.) The stalemate persisted through several papacies and several anti-papacies. Urban VI was succeeded by Boniface IX, Innocent VII, and Gregory XII. Clement VII, who had moved to Avignon, was succeeded by Benedict XIII.

The First John XXIII

In 1409, at the Council of Pisa, the interested par-ties tried to work things out, but things were made worse. The council declared both Gregory XII and Benedict XIII deposed, and it elected another claimant, Alexander V, who later was succeeded by John XXIII.[28]

Now there were three rival claimants to the papacy. Not wanting to see a fourth or fifth claimant, John XXIII called for a new council, which was held in Constance. This council obtained the resignations of John XXIII and Gregory XII. Benedict XIII, the anti-pope living in Avignon, refused to resign, but everyone ignored him, so the result was about the same.

The council elected Martin V[29] as pope, and that ended the schism. Confusion in the Church returned to its traditional level, to everyone's relief.

---

28 These two also were anti-popes, which is why, cen-turies later, Angelo Roncalli could call himself John XXIII, there not having been a legitimate pope of that name and number.

29 No relation to Martin of Tours. To avoid further mis-identification, no subsequent pope ever has taken the name Martin.

John Wycliffe

About this time there was a great nuisance in England. His name was John Wycliffe. He was a priest, theologian, philosopher, and precursor of the Protestant Reformation.

Wycliffe is remembered as an advocate of translating the Bible from the Latin Vulgate, the Church's official version, into the vernacular, in his case Middle English.

A vernacular translation was produced, but it never was clear how much, or how little, of it Wycliffe himself translated. Nevertheless, he got credit for the translation, such being the breaks of history, as already has been suggested.

Wycliffe's followers were called *Lollards* because the term *Wycliffers* sounded and looked awkward. They adopted beliefs attributed to Wycliffe, including iconoclasm and predestination, while rejecting the veneration of saints, transubstantiation, the sacrament of penance, monasticism, and the papacy.

This caused quite a ruckus in England. Wycliffe managed to escape retribution, if not blame, by conveniently dying from a stroke suffered on the Feast of the Holy Innocents, 1384.

In 1415 the Council of Constance declared Wycliffe a heretic and retroactively excommunicated him. There is no record of what Wycliffe thought of this.

Jan Hus

John Wycliffe's writings inspired the Czech reformer Jan Hus, who began his career as a professor at the University of Prague, where he promoted Wycliffe's ideas. This was in 1389, five years after the latter's death. Some years later Hus spoke out against indulgences. Shortly thereafter, three of his followers were shortened by being beheaded by the authorities. The three came to be considered the first martyrs of the future Hussite Church, but Hus himself ultimately came to be considered the chief martyr.

Hus attacked not only the papacy but the civil authorities who, being good Catholics, cooperated with the papacy. This gained Hus many new followers, including, eventually, the king of Bohemia, Wenceslas IV,[30] who often was at odds with the papacy.

Having the king on his side wasn't enough to keep Hus out of trouble, something he seemed always to be seeking. Eventually Hus was summoned to the Council of Constance. He was given a safe conduct guarantee by the king of Hungary, but the guarantee proved not to be so safe after all.

Hus repeatedly was asked to renounce his erroneous teachings, but he repeatedly declined. He was put on trial, found guilty of heresy, and handed over to the secular authorities, who had tired of his fomenting civil unrest.

They condemned Hus to death, and he was led to the stake that very day, which happened to be his birthday. The execution later was recognized by the Church to be A Great Blunder.

Not only was it unjust to Hus, but it paved the way for the Protestant Reformation, which was A Greater Blunder.

---

30 Not to be confused with Good King Wenceslas, a tenth-century martyr and saint made famous by a Christmas carol sung by Bing Crosby.

Joan of Ark

In fifteenth-century France a peasant girl named Joan claimed to receive visions of St. Michael the Archangel, St. Margaret, and St. Catherine. She asked for a meeting with the claimant to the French throne, the future Charles II, but repeatedly was rebuffed, until she wasn't. They had a chat, and he was impressed.

Joan was said to be a collateral descendant of Noah and thus was known as Joan of Ark. She became famous for leading a French army against the English and for wearing trousers. She was the first woman to do both simultaneously. The English took offense and burned her at the stake in 1431.

Joan's fashion did not catch on until exactly five centuries later, when Katharine Hepburn caused a stir in 1930s Hollywood by wearing trousers. Hepburn, unlike Joan, never was canonized because she never led a French army.

Fall of Byzantium

All this time, things were going from bad to worse in the East. In 1261 Michael Palaeologus had reconquered Constantinople from the Latins, who had taken over the city some years before. Michael tried to effect an ecclesiastical reunion with Rome, but Greek clerics and laymen balked. They still were bickering about the Filioque Clause, and Michael was denounced as a heretic. He died in 1281. With him went the last good prospects for reunion, at least for the next century and a half.

Byzantium continued a slow decline in political, military, and other terms. For a while, in the fifteenth

century, it looked like things might be patched up between the East and the West. Councils were held at Ferrara and Florence in 1438 and 1439, respectively.

The Greek representatives acceded to a bull that stated that the pope was the head of the Church, that the Holy Spirit proceeded from both the Father and the Son, and that it was valid to use either leavened or unleavened bread in the Eucharist.

These had been sticking points. Unfortunately, they continued to be sticking points when the folks back home learned what the Greek representatives had agreed to. The laity in Constantinople said, "Better the prophet's turban than the pope's tiara." They soon enough found out whether that was a smart switch.

In 1453 Constantinople fell to a Turkish army that was ten times as large as the army of the Byzantine emperor. Hagia Sophia, the main church of the Byzantine Empire, was converted to a mosque, and the patriarch of Constantinople became a puppet of the sultan. It was a Sad Day.

Alexander VI

In Rome, things were proceeding as usual: up and down, up and down. It came to be down's turn again when Alexander VI was elected pope in 1492. (The news so distressed Christopher Columbus that he left town and sailed westward.)[31]

Alexander belonged to the Borgia family, and that is why he was named a cardinal when only 25 years of age. Once pope, to solve persistent problems in Rome

---

31 See above, regarding the Reconquista and Columbus. He had multiple motives to cross the Atlantic.

and the Papal States, Alexander chose the customary way: nepotism. He installed his own family, including his several children, numerous nephews, and other dependents, into chief posts.

One of his sons was Cesare Borgia, whom he appointed as archbishop of Valencia when the lad was only 17. It is said that the Valencians were not impressed with Cesare, but of course they couldn't say so except *sotto voce*, which became a popular mode of speech.

Alexander's daughter was Lucrezia, whose name became legendary as legends of the Borgias multiplied. Her most famous deeds came much later, in twentieth-century films that she was unable to preview before their distribution to the general public.

Admittedly, there were other Renaissance popes of Alexander's low caliber, such as Julius II, but we will stop with this one example, on the principle that enough is enough. Except that we will mention that it was Julius, known as the "warrior pope" because he wielded a sword in battle, who wheedled Michelangelo into accepting the commission to paint the frescoes of the Sistine Chapel. Julius's works are nearly forgotten today, while Michelangelo's are universally revered, proving that the paintbrush is mightier than the sword.

Savonarola

Girolamo Savonarola was a Dominican friar who was considered the greatest preacher of the Italian Middle Ages, after Bernardine of Siena. By 1490 Savonarola was the prior of the famed San Marco monastery in Florence, which at the time was ruled by the Medici family, noted for its patronage of the arts and for its political and moral shenanigans.

The Medici were ousted by a citizens' rebellion in 1494. Savonarola took the opportunity to ratchet up the anti-corruption sermons that already had given him much influence over the populace. The Medici now gone, he focused his ire on the pope, Alexander VI, who, in another anticipation of Queen Victoria, was "not amused" by what he heard regarding the Florentine friar.

To get Savonarola to shut up, Alexander offered to make him a cardinal. Savonarola declined the honor, so the pope excommunicated him. In return, Savonarola invited the princes and kings of Europe to oust Alexander, on the grounds that the pope got his office through simony and therefore was illegitimate from the start. In this and other matters Savonarola claimed to be inspired directly by God, which was more than Alexander, for all his faults, ever claimed.

It wasn't long before Savonarola had effective control of Florence, even though he wasn't part of the city's government. And then, rather suddenly, he didn't have effective control.

He was arrested by the city government in 1498 and, with two of his friars, put on trial. The trial was perfunctory, as show trials always are, and the three were hanged in Piazza della Signoria, the main square of Florence. Their corpses were burned, and their ashes were thrown into the Arno, so their supporters could obtain no relics. Florence went back to its usual social and governmental corruption, and Savonarola went down in history as a holy hothead and a Public Nuisance.

The Renaissance

The Renaissance was an era of great artistic advancement. It was centered in Italy because that is where most of the great artists were, artists preferring warm climates to cold climates.[32]

It is said that Italy has half of all the fine art in Europe and that Florence has half of all the fine art in Italy. This may not be quite true arithmetically, but Florence made Michelangelo, Leonardo, and Botticelli household names, to the approval of the Florentine Travel Bureau.

Renaissance creativity extended even to architecture. Filippo Brunelleschi designed the dome over the cathedral of Florence. The dome was so massive that no one believed it could be built, but Brunelleschi built it anyway, to spite his critics, all of whom have gone into the dustbin of history.

Brunelleschi also discovered linear perspective. Until his time, objects in the backgrounds of paintings never looked right. Why no one before Brunelleschi realized this remains a mystery, but he fixed it. All connoisseurs of fine art have profited from Brunelleschi's perspective on perspective.

---

32 No Renaissance artists lived in Iceland, Greenland, or Scandinavia. Snow matters.

Period 4

The Modern Era

1500 Onward

Martin Luther

Martin Luther was not an unscrupulous monk. His problem was that he was too scrupulous. He suffered from scrupulosity. He always came away from confessing his sins wondering whether he had been sorry enough to have his sins forgiven. At length he got around this problem by doing away with confession, on the principle of "out of sight, out of mind."

Luther commonly is associated with indulgences, in a negative way. Admittedly, at the time there were abuses. A few itinerant priests who went around Germany preaching about indulgences tried to set up their own retirement funds by selling these remissions of temporal punishment. Church authorities condemned their practice, but condemnation often wasn't followed by enforcement.

Like others, Luther properly was annoyed at the situation, but, unlike others, he thought he found in Scripture proof that indulgences shouldn't be indulged in.

The more Luther studied Scripture and the more he looked around at the Church of his day, the more

he found things he didn't like, and the more modifications he wanted to make. Eventually he made a list called the 95 Theses and nailed the list to a church door in Wittenberg.

Luther as Editor

Without overtly using the title, Luther promoted himself to editor-in-chief of the Bible. Early on he decided that 2 Maccabees couldn't count as inspired Scripture because in chapter 12 it taught that "it is a holy and wholesome thought to pray for the dead, that they might be loosed from sins."

This verse implied not only that it is a good thing to pray for the dead (something Luther opposed, perhaps because he couldn't think of any dead people he had liked) but that some dead who were bound for heaven weren't there yet. In other words: purgatory (another something that Luther opposed).

To get around such awkward verses Luther jettisoned 2 Maccabees and other Old Testament books that contained material that didn't square with the way he would have inspired the Bible if he had been the Holy Spirit. This reduced his Old Testament from 46 books to 39.

Luther also didn't like the New Testament book of James, which he called an "epistle of straw" because that book promoted the idea that good works have something to do with salvation.

This violated Luther's conception of justification, which he thought was purely forensic—that is, you were justified (made righteous in God's eyes) if God pretended you were so, not because you actually had become so. This came to be known as the "faith alone" doctrine because, Luther said, an act of faith, by itself, was enough to become justified—and therefore saved. This novel theory of justification contradicted previous Christian teaching, but Luther didn't care because his theory made him feel better. As it turned out, he didn't get around to jettisoning the book of James from the Bible, having run out of blue pencils.

(As the Duke of Wellington, himself a one-time editor, later would say, "It was a near-run thing.")

Thomas More

Thomas More was famous for demonstrating that one should keep a prudent distance from kings. He had the misfortune of being friends with Henry VIII. (Something similar could be said of that king's six wives.)

The young More had considered entering a monastery, but instead he married and became active in politics, rising rapidly until Henry named him lord chancellor in 1529. It was a post More held for less than three years. He felt obliged to resign rather than to agree that Henry was the head of the Church in England and that the king's first marriage, to Catherine of Aragon, could be annulled.

Things were quiet until More declined to attend the coronation of Anne Boleyn as queen. This annoyed Henry, not to mention Anne, and More was brought up on charges of treason. He reiterated his position that the pope was the head of the Church wherever the Church might be found and that Henry still was married to Catherine and would be until her death.

This was intolerable, said the prosecutor. The hand-picked jury deliberated for all of fifteen minutes and found More guilty. Nobody was surprised, as nobody ever is surprised at the outcome of show trials. More was condemned to the chopping block. His execution took place in 1535 at Tower Hill. His last words, as he stood on the scaffold, were "I die the king's good servant but God's first." These words became so famous that they were made into a movie more than four centuries later. To this day no one can remember the last words of Henry VIII, and deservedly so.

An Established Church

Once More was out of the way, Henry VIII pursued other goals, such as acquiring another four wives (admittedly not simultaneously but successively) and for stumbling into the establishment of the Established Church, which in this case meant the Church of England, also known as the Anglican Church.

Like the future Smith Barney investment firm, Henry accomplished this the old-fashioned way: he earned it—or, more precisely, he bought off nobles with grants of cash and land that came from his appropriating Catholic Church property, particularly monasteries that he had suppressed and from which he had driven the monks and nuns.

The nobles became fantastically wealthy, nearly all of them deciding it was more enjoyable to be rich Anglicans than impoverished Catholics. They were the biggest supporters of Henry's new church and ended up building quaint countryside chapels that could be featured on picture postcards and in Victorian novels.

John Calvin

The year after Thomas More met his untimely end, John Calvin published the first edition of his *Institutes of the Christian Religion*, which came to be the manual of the branch of Protestantism known as Reformed Christianity or, more commonly, as Calvinism.

Himself French, Calvin was a minister in Geneva, Switzerland, where he famously preached more than two thousand sermons, most of them over an hour long.

He preached more than two hundred sermons on Deuteronomy alone, which was more than anyone thought ever could be preached on Deuteronomy. This feat was admired by everyone except those who sat through the sermons.

Calvin taught the complete depravity of man, an idea that contradicted the Catholic understanding of original sin, free will, and human nature, and he exaggerated predestination, which for him meant that some people, such as Calvin, were created precisely to go to heaven while others, such as those Calvin disagreed with, were created precisely to go to hell.

One of them was Michael Servetus, a Spaniard widely known for writing against the Trinity and, thus, for annoying both Catholics and Protestants.

In 1553 Servetus was on the run from Catholic authorities and tried to pass through Geneva incognito. He was found out anyway, was arrested, and was put on trial by the local Protestant government, over which Calvin had much influence.

Servetus was condemned as a heretic—which in fact he was, as everyone except Servetus agreed. He was burned at the stake, Calvin getting part of the credit and proving that the Swiss were as adept at lighting fires as were the Italians (Savonarola) and English (Joan).

Council of Trent

When it comes to being the all-time most influential general council, the title undoubtedly goes to the Council of Trent, held sporadically from 1545 to 1563 and called in response to the Protestant Reformation.

There were remarkably few bishops in attendance at Trent, which met in sessions separated by a fair number of years.

At the opening of the council, aside from the papal legates, there were only 32 bishops. During the remainder of this first period (1545-1547), the number of attending bishops rose to just 68. In the two sessions of the second period (1551-1552) there were 44 and 51 bishops. In the third period (1562-1563), the number rose to its highest point, 228. The concluding session of the council saw only 176 bishops.

These small numbers made for manageable discussions, which is why the council produced so much finely-honed text. The bishops could Get Things Done. The canons and decrees issued by them exceeded in volume the entire legislation of all eighteen prior general councils.[33]

---

33 Trent's volume would come to be dwarfed by that of Vatican II, the documents of which seem rambling by comparison. What else could one expect when "the committee of the whole" consisted of no fewer than 2,600 bishops? Only recently was it finally realized that, at some point during the four centuries between Trent and Vatican II, the Vatican had misplaced its entire cadre of line editors.

Trent's Reforms

Among many other reforms, Trent mandated that future priests be trained in seminaries. The custom had been that priests-to-be were trained by local priests in local parishes. This did not always have happy results, particularly when local priests themselves were poorly educated. (You can't teach what you don't know, as the saying goes.)

Seminaries became seminal parts of the Church from then on.

Trent dealt with doctrinal controversies raised by the Protestant Reformers. Among them was justification. The council fathers concluded that Luther's opinion on justification was unjustifiable. Likewise for other Protestant departures from perennial teaching.

The council reaffirmed that authentic teaching was not to be found only in Sacred Scripture but also in Tradition, that the sacraments actually were sacramental (conveying grace), not merely symbolic (conveying nothing), that purgatory was not only real but realistic (not everyone dying in the state of grace would be spiffed up enough for immediate entrance into heaven), and so on.

Trent also dealt with disciplinary and administrative issues. To the extent the Reformers had a point, it was that discipline often was lax and churchly administration often was disorganized.

For example, many bishops held more than one benefice: they lived in one diocese yet had control of other dioceses, which they seldom or never visited. Trent said this wouldn't do, and we ended up with the one bishop, one diocese policy that we enjoy (or not) today.

In retrospect, it came to be seen that the Council of Trent was so broad in its considerations and so precise in its formulations that, had it been held a century earlier, the Protestant Reformation likely would not have occurred.

Martin Luther would have ended his days as an over-scrupulous but otherwise forgotten monk—but that is something we never will know for sure, alternative history being even more confusing than actual history, as every historian will attest.

Pius V

Three years after the close of the Council of Trent, the new pope was Pius V. It was left to him to put the decrees of the council into practice, and he did such a good job of it that he was the last pope to be canonized until Pius X, who reigned three and a half centuries later.

Pius V is remembered for having revised the *Missale Romanum*, for suppressing variants of the Mass that were relatively new at the time while permitting variants of long standing, and for putting the lid on liturgical changes for the next four hundred years.

He organized a crusade that repelled the Turkish attack on Italy, and he was able to cajole Catholic monarchs to fund and equip a fleet, headed by Don Juan of Austria, that defeated the Turks at the sea battle of Lepanto in 1571. Credit for the victory went not just to Don Juan and Pius but to the Virgin Mary, since the pope had arranged for countless rosaries to be said throughout Catholic Europe on the fleet's behalf.

Not all of Pius's actions had the results one might have wished. In 1570 he issued a decree deposing

Queen Elizabeth,[34] daughter of Henry VIII, for heresy and persecution of Catholics in England. The only thing that came from it was increased persecution of Catholics.

On a happier note, it was Pius who got credit for popes wearing white, the story being that, since he had been a Dominican, he was used to wearing white and saw no reason to change colors. In fact, popes before his time had worn white, but none of them got credit for starting the tradition, such being the breaks of sartorial history.

Hernán Cortés

Hernán Cortés was a Spanish conquistador who led an expedition that resulted in the military and spiritual conquest of Mexico. From 1519 to 1521 his small army marched on and ultimately defeated the Aztecs at their capital, Tenochtitlan, which later became known as Mexico City because it was a city in Mexico.

The king of the Aztecs was Montezuma. He was held in high regard by his fellow Aztecs and in somewhat lower regard by members of other indigenous tribes, many of whom were rounded up and became human sacrifices at Tenochtitlan's main temple, sometimes up to thousands of victims per day.

Not surprisingly, the victims strenuously objected to having their hearts ripped out of their living bodies, but Montezuma didn't care because he was a heartless man.

The non-Aztec tribes, seeing their chance, allied themselves with the Spaniards, and at length the Aztec

---

34 The first one, not the nice one.

empire was overthrown and Montezuma was killed, apparently by his own men, and good riddance.

Cortés wasn't just interested in military conquest. A devout Catholic, he asked the king of Spain to send missionaries, and the king did so, sending many Franciscans and some Dominicans. They proved to be effective evangelists.

Everybody except the former Aztec leadership thought the Catholic faith was A Big Step Up.

Our Lady of Guadalupe

In 1531 the missionaries in Mexico got help from an unexpected quarter.

A Mexican farmer named Juan Diego had a vision of the Virgin Mary, who came to be known locally as Our Lady of Guadalupe even though the town of Guadalupe was in Spain and not in Mexico.

As confusing as the geography might be, the apparition not surprisingly got Juan Diego's immediate attention and, soon enough, the attention of Church authorities.

Then it got the attention of just about everyone in Mexico but not, so far as is known, of many people in Guadalupe, Spain. (Such are the breaks of history, as repeatedly has been noted.)

Conversions in Mexico multiplied rapidly, and they extended ultimately to the rest of Latin America. During those years the Catholic Church in Europe lost many members to the Protestant Reformation, but that loss was more than compensated for by the number of converts made in the Western Hemisphere, proving that You Can't Keep a Good Religion Down.

Francis Xavier

Conversions didn't happen only in the West. They also happened in the East. Many of them were the work of Francis Xavier. A native of Navarre, Spain, he was a friend of Ignatius Loyola and was, like Ignatius, one of the first seven Jesuits. Unlike Ignatius, he was a traveling man.

(This is not to say that Ignatius didn't travel, but, like everyone else in Spain, he was sedentary compared to Francis.)

Starting in 1541, Francis traveled to Goa and other parts of India, to Southeast Asia, to Japan, and to China. He racked up more frequent sailing miles than any missionary of his time.

On his travels Francis took only a few books, including a catechism, a breviary, and *Instructions on How to Lead a Virtuous Life* by Marko Marulić, a native of Split and Croatia's top writer of the Renaissance.[35]

On his first journey, Francis left Lisbon for Goa, which was a Portuguese colony. During several years there and in neighboring places he built forty churches and made many converts, but he thought he could do better elsewhere, so he left for Japan, where he made thousands of converts in less than three years.

He never mastered the Japanese language, but he had the fortuitous assistance of a Japanese convert who acted as his interpreter, thus proving that God Provides.

---

35 This now-obscure man is mentioned here because the Author's maternal grandparents immigrated to the U.S. from Split. If you are an Author, you may insert as many irrelevancies into your text as you wish. This is known in law as The Author's Privilege.

Learning that the Japanese looked up to the culture of China,[36] Francis next traveled to that country, thinking that if he could convert the Chinese, the conversion of the Japanese would be made easier. It made sense, but Francis never had a chance to find out whether it was so, because he died shortly after reaching China.

Eventually his body was moved to Goa, but his right forearm was taken to Rome, where it is displayed in Il Gesù, the Jesuit Church. Another arm bone went to Macau. No record exists of what Francis thought of this distribution of his remains.

Galileo

Galileo Galilei, despite his surname, was not from Galilee. He was from Pisa, which is about the same thing, if you're a Pisan. At the time, Pisa was part of the duchy of Florence, which is why the museum dedicated to Galileo's works is found in the latter city rather than in the city of his birth. Galileo was a physicist and engineer, but he also was an astronomer, which is all he is remembered as today.

For centuries, opponents of the Church have claimed that the Galileo Case shows that the Church has been hostile to science. Interestingly (but not to these opponents, it seems), it is the only case ever cited that purports to show the alleged hostility, because in every other interaction between the Church and science the two have been shown to be friends.

A century prior to Galileo's time, another astronomer, Nicolaus Copernicus of Poland, argued that the

---

36 This is decidedly not the situation today, but that is another story.

Sun, rather than the Earth, is the center of the solar system, which made perfect sense, because otherwise it all along would have been called the global system, which it never was. Church bigwigs thought so highly of Copernicus's work that a cardinal funded the scientist's research out of his own pocket.

Galileo differed from Copernicus in that he imagined that not only was he an accomplished astronomer but an accomplished exegete of the Bible, which he wasn't. Copernicus simply reported his scientific observations and conclusions drawn from them. He didn't get into trouble. Galileo claimed his similar conclusions, based on similar observations, were taught by Holy Writ. He thus stepped into the realm of the theologians, who didn't want him there.

Galileo didn't make things better for himself when he published, in 1632, the *Dialogue Concerning the Two Chief World Systems*.[37] He named the character defending the opposite point of view "Simplicio," which was bad enough since it looked like "Simpleton," but he seemed to put the pope's own words into the mouth of that character, which was worse.[38]

That was enough to bring Galileo before the Inquisition. The verdict was that he was found "suspect of heresy" and that he would have to spend the rest of his life under house arrest, which he did, though in a rather comfortable way.

---

37 The two systems were geocentrism and heliocentrism. Some years ago the former made something of a comeback in Christian circles, until your Author wrote a book against it, *The New Geocentrists*. Geocentrists haven't been heard from since.

38 Unsurprisingly, Galileo never was considered for the diplomatic corps.

Jansenism

Jansenism was a heresy named, conveniently, after Cornelius Jansen, a Dutch Catholic theologian. He died in 1638, before the heresy got off the ground, which meant he wasn't around to see the heresy's effects, which were long lasting.

Jansen left behind the manuscript of a book, published in 1640 as *Augustinus*. It was his understanding of the teachings of Augustine of Hippo (the Augustine mispronounced in Florida).

The main problem with Jansen's theorizing lay in his belief that grace was irresistible. Free will had no part in accepting grace, he claimed. If God wanted to send grace your way, you were stuck with it. This made grace the only kind of gift that one couldn't decline.

There were other problems in Jansen's book, such as the claim that it was heretical to say that Christ died for all. In fact, there were so many problems that the book was condemned by the Holy Office in 1642, which was quick action on Rome's part.

Of all the heresies to inflict the Church, Jansenism might be the one exhibiting the most sustained equivocating by its leadership. Each time a Jansenist proposition was condemned, the leaders said, "But we don't believe *that*, exactly." They kept this up for decades. Politicians throughout the world learned from them.

By the second half of the eighteenth century Jansenism no longer was promoted by anyone of note, but some of its ideas persisted into the twentieth century, such as that one should not receive Communion often—a proposition condemned by Pius X, who said just the opposite.

Quietism

Contemporary with Jansenism in its early years was another heresy internal to the Church, Quietism. Its promoters were anything but quiet, because they imagined that they had The True Spiritual Way.

Quietism was founded by Miguel de Molinos, a Spanish priest. He taught that, if you wanted to advance in the spiritual life, you needed to be entirely passive to grace. This meant no thinking about spiritual matters and no physical actions that might promote a receptive attitude, as all that was hostile to grace. You were supposed to just sit there. As a logical consequence, all prayer was to be contemplative only.

That eliminated set prayers, such as the Our Father, which had been set by Christ himself and which had had a long run of popularity, and for good reason. It also meant that you should avoid acts of virtue, since they distracted one from being purely contemplative.[39]

Eventually Quietism was condemned by the pope, and in 1687 Molinos was degraded from the priesthood and had to spend the rest of his life in a monastery, where, unsurprisingly, he was not known for being talkative.

The Popish Plot

The Popish Plot was a plot that didn't exist. It was invented in 1678 by Titus Oates, a man who did exist. He claimed that Catholics in England were plotting to

---

39 It would seem that eating also would distract one from being purely contemplative, but there is no evidence that Molinos declined his dinners. Such are the inconsistencies within heresies.

assassinate the king, Charles II. With the help of a fanatically anti-Catholic clergyman, Oates wrote a long dossier that outlined the plot, but not a line of the dossier was true. That didn't matter. The document ignited a firestorm of indignation, and many Catholics were accused of treason. Nine Jesuit priests were executed, and a dozen more died in prison. Other priests were arrested, as were many Catholic laymen. Catholics as a whole were commanded to move out of London.

Eventually, during the reign of James II, Titus Oates himself was arrested and tried for perjury, but he got off lightly compared to the people who went to the gallows because of his lies.

Such, alas, are the breaks of Judicial Inconsistency, another thing known by every historian.

James II

James II became the king of England in 1685. He had a couple of things going against him: first, being Catholic in a nation that had become strongly anti-Catholic; second, his personality.

He might have had a long reign if his diplomatic skills had been better, but they weren't much. He was obstinate and had quite a temper, neither a virtue when what was needed was delicacy when trying to improve the lot of English Catholics.

James was a convert to the faith. Upon ascending the throne, he immediately dispensed Catholics from all legal disabilities, which was a good thing in theory, but he should have taken his time about it, which would have been a better thing in practice and might have preserved the throne for him.

Pope Innocent XI, who was not so innocent of the ways of the world as his name might suggest, warned James to proceed with caution, but James wasn't one to take advice. The king bungled ahead, alienating sympathetic Protestant leaders, both religious and civil.

When it was announced that James's Catholic wife, Mary of Modena, gave birth to a son (later known as the Old Pretender because he pretended to be king when he wasn't), there was an uprising of the nobility. They arranged for William of Orange, the husband of James's oldest daughter, Mary (born of James's previous wife, a Protestant), to take over the throne.

When nearly everyone seemed to back William over James, the king booked with Cunard and left England for France. This was called the Glorious Revolution, but it wasn't glorious for James, his wife, or his son, who also was named James.[40]

It also wasn't glorious for Catholics who might be in line for the throne. In 1701 Parliament passed the Act of Succession, which excluded Catholics and anyone married to a Catholic from becoming the monarch. Catholics remained second-class citizens well into the nineteenth century and didn't become first-class citizens until British Protestants no longer cared much about Protestantism.

Edict of Nantes

Although Protestants of the sixteenth century lived mainly in Germany, Switzerland, and Britain, a fair

---

40 Known as James III, the son tried, some years later, to regain the throne for the Stuart line but failed. *His* son was Bonnie Prince Charlie, known as the Young Pretender because he was younger than his father.

number of them lived in France, where they were known as Huguenots. They professed a variant of Calvinism.

In 1596 the French king, Henry IV, issued the Edict of Nantes, which gave the Huguenots civil and religious rights, so long as they stayed in and around their own cities, which mainly were in the west and south of France. The king did this because he had grown tired of religious strife between Catholics and Protestants.

This toleration worked well enough, until one of Henry's successors grew intolerant of it.

In 1685 Louis XIV revoked the Edict of Nantes and ordered the destruction of Huguenot churches and schools and the exile of Huguenot ministers. In the future, he said, Huguenot children were to be educated only in Catholic schools. The king's motive was to unify the people of France, but his plan backfired, as plans of politicians often do.

Louis was known as the Sun King, but tens of thousands of Huguenots, seeing that he didn't have a sunny disposition, fled France for other countries, where their embittered descendants became enemies of the French monarchy and willing cooperators with the later French Revolution, during which Louis' grandson lost not only his kingdom but his head, proving, as Richard Weaver later noted, that Ideas Have Consequences.[41]

Freemasonry

Scholars say that Freemasonry began in 1717, when several prominent British men left an existing society

---

41 Actions have consequences too, as any constable will affirm.

that purported to be a medieval guild and started a new organization that substituted Deism for sectarian Protestantism. They called the new movement Freemasonry because there was no initiation fee.

Soon there were Freemasons in France, Germany, Portugal, Holland, Switzerland, Denmark, and even Italy. Their local clubhouses were called *lodges* because that term didn't sound as juvenile as *clubhouses*, and these were serious men. They were so serious that they replicated the secret handshakes and passwords of the clubhouses they used to belong to as boys.

In truth, Freemasonry was less than watered down Christianity. It wasn't Christianity at all. It spoke of a Great Architect of the Universe, but that personage could not be identified as any Person of the Trinity. Freemasons denied the supernatural order and, as a logical consequence, were opposed to Christianity in general and Catholicism in particular, the latter being the most supernatural version of Christianity because it was the truest.

As early as 1738 Pope Clement XII condemned Freemasonry, and his condemnation was repeated repeatedly by later popes. Unfortunately, this didn't eliminate Freemasonry from Catholic lands, not a few high-ranking clerics being fooled into becoming Freemasons, demonstrating that native intelligence was not a prerequisite for ecclesiastical advancement.

New Religious Orders

The thirteenth century saw the founding of important religious orders, such as the Dominicans and the Franciscans. Another century in the same league was the eighteenth, which saw the founding of the Christian Brothers, the Passionists, and the Redemptorists.

The Christian Brothers were founded by John de La Salle, a French priest. The members, who were devoted to education, were laymen rather than priests and thus were called brothers. Since they also happened to be Christians, the name became Christian Brothers. (What else could it have been?)

The Passionists were passionate about asceticism. Their rule required them to abstain for three days each week and to practice severe austerity in dress and lodging. They were active in preaching, not something easy to do when one is on a perpetual diet. Their founder was a former soldier who took the name Paul of the Cross. He was an Italian, but his order had, as a special task, the conversion of England. The most notable success was with John Henry Newman, who was received into the Church by a Passionist priest.

The Redemptorists were founded by Alphonsus Liguori, whose curious surname led some people to think he had a connection to the distilling of spirits. His order focused on the salvation of the poor, many of whom needed to be weaned from distilled spirits, so maybe his surname was providential.

Benedict XIII

When the papacy fell vacant in 1724, at the death of Innocent XIII, the resultant conclave was a protracted one, lasting two months. The cardinals just couldn't make up their minds.

Impatient to return to his diocese of Benevento, one of the cardinals, Pietro Orsini, decided to pray a novena in hopes of a prompt resolution. A prompt resolution is what he got, but it was not the resolution he expected: he was elected and took the name Benedict XIII, proving that prayer always is answered, sometimes with a "Yes," sometimes with a "No," and sometimes with a "Yes, but—surprise!"

Junípero Serra

The Jesuits were active in missionary work in the Far East, but in the Far West, which is to say the Western Hemisphere, most of the missionary work was done by Franciscans. One of the most effective was Junípero Serra. His given name had been Miguel, but when he became a Franciscan friar he took the name of a tree, for reasons that remain obscure.[42]

Serra traveled to Mexico, teaching and preaching there for several years. It was a hard life but not hard enough for him, so he wore a hairshirt. Hairshirts were popular in those days but have fallen out of fashion.[43] Serra's strict self-discipline prepared him for the hard life of being a missionary in California. (Even today being a missionary in California is a hard life, but for different reasons.)

Serra established California's first Franciscan mission at San Diego in 1769, and he went on to establish eight more. Eventually there were 21 in the state. He often, and erroneously, gets credit for establishing all

---

42 One might think that Serra would have become the patron saint of horticulturalists, but that role already was taken by Fiacre, a seventh-century Irish saint, which is odd, because nothing but potatoes will grow in Ireland and even then not always, as the Potato Famine suggests.

43 For which the Author is grateful.

of them. Such are the breaks of misconstrued architectural history, as every historian knows.

The French Revolution

The French Revolution broke out in 1789 and went through several phases. In 1792 there were widespread massacres of people who didn't want to revolt. Four hundred priests were killed, and up to forty thousand clergy fled France.

The next year King Louis XVI was executed, and after that things really got bad with the Terror, which lasted through 1794. (This was called Rationalism.) Eventually the revolutionaries turned upon one another, there being no other fresh targets for their attacks. A long line of revolutionaries, such as Maximilien Robespierre, went to the guillotines, and no one was surprised, least of all Robespierre.

In 1798 a French revolutionary army invaded Italy and took Pius VI captive. The octogenarian pope was taken to France, where he died the next year. This episode was a tremendous blunder by the revolutionaries, who apparently forgot the French adage *"qui mange du pape meurt,"* which means "whoever eats the pope dies." Four days before the death of Pius, Napoleon Bonaparte left Egypt, where he had headed an army, and made for France, where he ended up overthrowing the revolutionary government, seized power for himself, and became the first modern dictator.

Napoleon

Napoleon was a man short of stature but long on ambition. He wanted to control the Church, but he kept in

mind how *mange* could lead to *meurt*. He was unsuccessful in preventing the election of a new pope. Pius VII was chosen by a conclave that met on one of the Venetian islands, Rome still being in control of the French. The pope was able to go to Rome a few months later. He ended up having a long reign, 1800-1823.

Eventually Napoleon agreed to a concordat with the Holy See, and the Church was re-established in France, though the number of clergy was only about a third of what it had been before the revolution.

In 1809 a French army was in Rome again, and Pius was arrested. He was taken to Savona, not far from the French border, where he was kept under guard. He excommunicated everyone involved in his detention, including Napoleon, but Napoleon didn't care because he wasn't a Catholic except when it was convenient for him. The pope was kept incommunicado and was permitted few visitors. This didn't bother him especially, since he always had been a simple, humble man, having been a monk before his election.

In 1812 everything collapsed for Napoleon. His army was defeated in Russia by General Winter, and by 1814 Pius was back in Rome—and Napoleon's men weren't. The *meurt* had caught up with the *mange*, to the amusement of everyone except Napoleon.

Anti-Catholicism in the U.S.

Anti-Catholic sentiment was strong in the U.S. in the early part of the nineteenth century. This sentiment was a response to the large number of Catholic immigrants who were coming to America. Several newspapers were launched precisely to oppose the

"Romanism" of the immigrants. Among them were *The Boston Recorder*, a Baptist publication called *The Christian Watchman*, and a weekly called *The Protestant*. These and other newspapers published lurid tales about the Catholic Church, particularly about priests and nuns. Everything was a fabrication, but that didn't matter to the readership, which lapped up anything anti-Catholic.

A future archbishop, a puckish priest named John Hughes, submitted fantastical stories to these newspapers under an alias, and then he delighted Catholics and disconcerted Protestants by discrediting the newspapers for having run such nonsense.[44]

Anti-Catholic screeds didn't appear only in newspapers. They also appeared in books. One of the most widely read was *Foreign Conspiracy Against the Liberties of the United States*. The author was Samuel F. B. Morse, inventor of the telegraph and developer of the Morse Code.

In 1836 Morse ran for mayor of New York as the candidate of the Nativist Party. He received only 1,496 votes, out of about fifty thousand eligible voters. Perhaps surprisingly, he couldn't even attract votes from Protestants. Later, when he visited Rome, Morse refused to remove his hat in the presence of the pope. The pope, being an adult, didn't care.

Gregory XVI

Gregory XVI, who reigned from 1831 to 1846, was said to be the most reactionary pope of modern times. He

---

44 Catholics always have known how to have fun. It's built in to their religion.

stood athwart history yelling, "Stop!", but it didn't, as it usually doesn't.

It was Gregory who forbade gas lighting to be installed on the streets of Rome, and he forbade railroads to be built in the Papal States. These measures forced people to walk in the daytime, which proved good for their waistlines. This was biblical and promoted safety, Christ having said, "Anyone who walks in the daytime will not stumble" (John 11:9). In this way Gregory unknowingly laid the groundwork for our own era's obsession with fitness. Another quirk of history.

Still another, one that might surprise his detractors: in 1839 Gregory issued an apostolic letter that denounced the transatlantic slave trade, proving he was not so reactionary after all.

Pius IX

Pius IX succeeded Gregory XVI in 1846. Inasmuch as Gregory had been thought a reactionary, everyone assumed that Pius had to be a liberal. Everyone was in for a surprise.

At first it did seem that Pius would loosen things up, at least in his civil role as head of the Papal States, but then the insurrections of 1848 occurred all over Europe, and Pius decided that the loosening up was over. He thereafter became considered a very conservative pope but not a reactionary one, since that title belonged exclusively to Gregory.

It was during Pius's reign that Italy became a unified country for the first time since there were Roman emperors.

Little by little, small Italian kingdoms and princedoms were gobbled up by Giuseppe Garibaldi's army, until the only one remaining outside the control of King Victor Emmanuel was the Papal States, which included not just Rome but a large swath of the central part of the Italian peninsula.

Eventually, in 1870, after the Italian regime had taken control even of most of the Papal States, Rome itself fell to the Italian army, and thereafter Pius confined himself to the 109 acres of Vatican City, becoming what he termed "the prisoner of the Vatican."

The takeover brought an abrupt end to the general council that had been called the previous year.

Pius reigned a long time, until 1878. The only pope to reign longer was the first pope, Peter, who would have reigned longer yet if it hadn't been, as noted near the beginning of this book, that someone finked on him.

Vatican I

As just mentioned, Vatican I was a truncated general council. It accomplished only part of what had been planned, due to the unsettled political situation in Italy.

Pius IX thought it was okay if he got stuck as "the prisoner of the Vatican," but the other bishops at Vatican I didn't want to get stuck there too, not having rooms as nice as those in the Apostolic Palace, so they all went home, and that ended the council.

The remote impetus for the council was the French Revolution, which had overturned the established order in Europe. When Pope Pius VI died in 1799, a prisoner of the French regime, many people thought the

Catholic Church was finished, but, as G. K. Chesterton later would write, the funeral was interrupted by the least expected thing: the corpse came back to life.

Popes who followed Pius VI did their best to resuscitate the Church in Europe, and on the whole they did a good job. For example, in 1850 Pius IX was able to re-establish Catholic dioceses and bishops in England. English Protestants called it the "Papal Aggression," but English Catholics called it about time.

People of all persuasions and none were interested when Pius IX issued, in 1869, a call for a new general council, the first since the Council of Trent. Vatican I was attended by 744 bishops, about two hundred of them from Italy, where there still prevailed the ancient custom that each city should have its own bishop. (This seemed fine to the Italians, but Catholics in other cities felt shortchanged. The Italians didn't care.)

The main task of Vatican I was to define the infallibility of the pope. This is not to be confused with the impeccability of the pope, which no one who has paid the least attention to Catholic history ever has believed in.[45] A substantial minority of the bishops at the council—something between one hundred and two hundred bishops—thought it "inopportune" to define papal infallibility. These bishops became known, in the copious literature that followed, as the Inopportunists. They thought it would be better to take up the topic later, such as in the twenty-third century.

In the end, only two bishops voted against the decree on papal infallibility. Immediately after the vote, both of them indicated their acceptance of the

45 Earliest example of the popes' non-impeccability: Peter's triple denial. Need we go on?

teaching. One of these bishops was Edward Fitzgerald, the bishop of Little Rock, Arkansas. His (temporary) opposition came to be known historically as the Little Rock vs. the Big Rock.

John Henry Newman

John Henry Newman was the Smartest Man in England in the nineteenth century. He had been a minister in the Anglican Church but, after years of careful study of the Fathers of the Church (all of whom, as mentioned earlier, were Catholics), he realized that he had signed up with the wrong institution.

He switched and became Catholic in 1845, and for his troubles he was made a cardinal, but not until 34 years later, Rome being slow about such things back then.[46] Newman's most widely read book has been *Apologia Pro Vita Sua*, an account of the development of his religious opinions. It has sold well, but it would have sold better had the title been in English. The publisher should have foreseen that by the centenary of Newman's death (he died in 1890) almost no one in America (or in England, for that matter) would be able to understand the Latin title, which could have been rendered as *A Defense of His Life* or, if a savvy marketing department had been consulted, as *Why I'm Right and You're Not*.

In the minds of scholars, Newman's most important book was *An Essay on the Development of Christian Doctrine*. From the start it had an English title, but that

---

46 Actually, it was more than that. Pius IX had reservations about Newman, proving that papal infallibility didn't extend to judgments of men's worth. The year after Pius died, his successor, Leo XIII, offered Newman the red hat.

wasn't why it was his most important book. It was his most important book because he showed that Catholic beliefs and practices of the nineteenth century, and the Church itself, could be traced all the way back to the earliest centuries of Christianity—and that distinctive Protestant teachings and Protestant churches couldn't.

This proved rather embarrassing for Protestants, which is why Newman's *Essay* has not been included on student reading lists at Protestant seminaries. (Who can blame them?)

Baltimore Catechism

Three times in the nineteenth century the Catholic bishops of America met in plenary session in Baltimore, which was the top American see. At their third meeting, in 1884, they decided to produce a series of catechism texts for children.

These began to appear the next year and were called the *Baltimore Catechism* even though they were intended mainly for children living outside that city. The books went through several editions before being formalized early in the twentieth century.

There ended up being three texts, of increasing length and broken into grade levels. *Baltimore Catechism No. 1* was for first communicants through fifth graders. *Baltimore Catechism No. 2* was for sixth graders through ninth graders and for those preparing for confirmation. *Baltimore Catechism No. 3* was for those already confirmed and for high schoolers.

That's as far as the catechisms went, because it was expected that by the end of high school a young person would know everything about the faith, which nearly was true, at least compared to today, when Catholic students finishing even Catholic high schools generally know less than was contained in *Baltimore Catechism No. 1*, further proof of the decline of education even within the Church.

Each volume consisted of questions and answers. In the original, unitary edition of 1885 there were 421 questions. The three subsequent volumes ended up with fewer questions, but there still were many questions in each volume. The number of answers exactly equaled the number of questions, the editors having done their work well.

In the 1960s, in a fit of optimism, the *Baltimore Catechism* was dropped from Catholic instructional programs, including parochial schools, and Catholics in America reverted to the religious ignorance enjoyed by their eighteenth-century forebears. This was called Educational Progress.

Leo XIII

In 1891 Pope Leo XIII issued *Rerum Novarum,* the earliest and most important of the modern social encyclicals. Nearly every pope since his time has issued one or more social encyclicals, this having become a popular pastime with popes.

Rerum Novarum appeared in English under various titles, such as *On the Condition of Labor*. The encyclical was prompted by the sorrier aspects of the Industrial Revolution, and Leo was eager to affirm the rights and duties both of laborers and employers.

This was welcomed by all laborers and by two or three employers.

The pope promoted the principle of subsidiarity as he condemned socialism, which was a large problem at that time and later. Socialism held that everything should be controlled by the state, while subsidiarity held that things should be controlled at the lowest possible social level: the family first, then local associations (including the Church), then municipalities, and eventually upward to the state, which should be last on the list.

Leo affirmed that the state had an important role to play in society, but his words disappointed most legislators, given their impressions of how important they themselves were.

Pius X

Leo's successor was Pius X, whose given name was Giuseppe Sarto. His surname meant *tailor*, but his father was a postman. The discrepancy never has been explained.

Pius X was the last pope to be canonized until canonizing popes became fashionable once more in the twenty-first century, and he had been the only pope to be canonized since Pius V.

He wrote against Modernism, the religious theory that everything, whether doctrinal or moral, is adjustable to suit one's preferences.

Modernism was popular for years, but today the only self-described Modernists to be found are gray-haired. Young people genuinely interested in Catholicism think Modernism is too old-fashioned.[47] Pius himself is considered old-fashioned by some, but

47 Which is true, as smart historians know.

such people are at a loss for words when they learn that Pius called for the laity's "active participation" in the liturgy, half a century before Vatican II was convened.[48]

This pope is remembered particularly for calling for frequent reception of Holy Communion and for lowering the age of First Communion.

Like his immediate predecessor, Pius called for an expanded study of Thomism, particularly as an antidote to the many philosophical errors that had arisen in the nineteenth century.

On his accession to the Throne of Peter, Pius declined to make his impoverished sisters papal countesses. This shocked Roman High Society, and just as well, since High Societies regularly need shocking.

Benedict XV

Pius X died three weeks after World War I began. That war was supposed to be "the war to end war," but it wasn't, and later it was called the Great War, even though there wasn't anything great about it except for the extent of its destruction, which greatly exceeded anything the belligerents originally had imagined would occur, proving again the shortsightedness of politicians.

Pius's successor, Benedict XV, tried repeatedly and fruitlessly to bring the war to an end.

He adopted a position of strict impartiality, but each side in the war thought he was partial to the other side, which itself proved his impartiality. Unfortunately, leaders of the warring powers all wanted Absolute

---

48 Another example of Cognitive Dissonance.

Victory[49] instead of peace through compromise, so they rejected Benedict's interventions.

Fatima

In 1917 three peasant children in the small town of Fatima, Portugal, claimed to have seen an apparition of the Virgin Mary.

Clever people thought the children were just being clever and amusing and so didn't believe them, but people who didn't consider themselves to be clever did believe the children.

The children returned to the site of the original apparition monthly, and each time they went, the curious crowd grew. The children said that at the final apparition there would be a miracle. Since everyone likes to watch miracles, people came from far and wide to view whatever was going to happen.

About seventy thousand people were on hand, including officials of the government, which was anti-clerical, and reporters from newspapers, which were even more anti-clerical than the government.

The officials, being officious, and the reporters, being smart, knew that nothing was going to happen, and they wanted to see the expressions on the faces of the yokels when, in fact, nothing happened.

Except something happened.

Everyone saw what appeared to be a dancing sun. The reporters, who at least were minimally honest, reported that they saw what everyone else claimed to see.

---

49 What the leaders absolutely got was another war two decades later.

The government officials hemmed and hawed, which is what government officials do when they don't have an explanation for something.

Everyone else was impressed, which seemed quite appropriate under the circumstances, miracles being impressive, especially flashy ones.

Pius XI

Benedict XV was succeeded by Pius XI in February 1922. The new pope was happy to take on a new name, since his surname had been Ratti, which is Italian for *rats*. He considered the papacy a step up, at least in terms of nomenclature.

He had lived a relatively retired life until he was in his sixties. He spent years working as a theology professor and then worked at the Vatican Library. In his free time he was an incessant mountain climber.[50] He was named the cardinal archbishop of Milan only a year before being elected pope.

At his election he re-instituted a custom that had fallen into desuetude since 1870: he appeared on the balcony of St. Peter's Basilica to give the annual *Urbi et Orbi* blessing. In the large crowd was a fellow named Mussolini, who was a member of the Chamber of Deputies[51] and who took note of the pope's popularity and thus toned down his own anti-clericalism.

In 1929 the Holy See signed the Lateran Treaty with the Fascist government of Italy. The treaty made Vatican City a separate country, which it had not been

---

50 Thus endearing himself to the Author.

51 Later that year Mussolini became prime minister, to everyone's ultimate dissatisfaction.

since 1870. This meant the pope no longer was "the prisoner of the Vatican." This was good for Pius. He now could travel outside the Vatican, but he never had the chance to climb another mountain, except for symbolic ones.

In 1937 Pius issued the only papal encyclical to be written in German, *Mit Brennender Sorge*. It was a strong condemnation of Nazism.[52] That same year he also issued *Divini Redemptoris*, which condemned Communism.[53]

Pius XII

Pius XI was succeeded in 1939 by Pius XII, which made mathematical sense. The new pope had been a Vatican diplomat and secretary of state under Pius XI, and Europe in particular and the world in general were in much need of diplomacy.

A new and more violent war broke out later that year, and Pius XII, like Benedict XV, urged a quick, negotiated resolution. As with Benedict, Pius was ignored by politicians on all sides, something commonly done in wartime since politicians never find themselves in the line of fire.

Pius issued many important documents during his reign, such as *Mystici Corporis Christi*, which explained the true nature of the Church; *Humani Generis*, which warned against still-present errors of Modernism; and *Divino Afflante Spiritu*, which encouraged deeper biblical studies.

---

52 At which point Pius was dropped from Hitler's Christmas card list.

53 At which point Stalin modified his Christmas card list too.

In 1950 Pius exercised the rarely used charism of papal infallibility when he defined definitively the Assumption of the Virgin Mary, something that Catholics had assumed to be true and now didn't need to harbor any doubts about.[54]

Catholic Apologetics Revived

The first half of the twentieth century saw the rise of lay-run apologetics, particularly in the English-speaking world. Before this, apologetics largely had been a clerical pastime, but many Catholic laymen thought it was past time for laymen to get involved, as they had been involved in the earliest centuries of the Church.[55]

The premier Catholic apologetics organization was the Catholic Evidence Guild, founded in London in 1918.

By the middle of the next decade the Guild was headed by Frank Sheed, an immigrant from Australia, and his wife, Maisie Ward, not an immigrant from Australia but rather a descendant of one of England's premier Catholic families.[56] (As a side venture, the two established a publishing house that sported their surnames.)

---

54 Not that many of them had any doubts about the doctrine, but just in case.

55 Justin Martyr being a good example: he was a layman, not a priest.

56 Her grandfather was William George Ward, who was famous for saying that he wanted to have a papal bull delivered each morning along with his copy of the *London Times*. All he ever got, though, was the newspaper. He died a frustrated man.

Sheed, Ward, and their compatriots had considerable success in explaining the faith not just to Catholics but also to non-Catholics. They made many converts on both sides of the Atlantic. Among their allies was Arnold Lunn, who converted to Catholicism in 1933 and who went on to become a noted apologist in his own right.[57]

By the early 1950s apologetics had fallen out of fashion and in some quarters even was looked down upon, chiefly by people unable to frame an argument on any topic whatsoever—another consequence of the decline of public and even of Catholic education.

A generation later apologetics began to make a comeback, beginning in California (of all places) and extending outward from there.[58]

History Stops

This book now has reached the second half of the twentieth century, at which point the Author of these pages entered the world and Church history stopped, at least for him. Nothing further can count as history for him while he yet lives, because history is stuff in the dead past, and he is not dead yet.

Once he departs this Vale of Tears, his literary executors will endeavor to bring this book current to the year of his passing. Until then, so far as he is concerned, Catholic history is in suspense.

As, in a way, it always has been.

---

57 Lunn was an accomplished alpine skier and invented the slalom ski race. Most skiers never knew about his apologetics work, much to their loss.

58 The revival was due in small part to a dull fellow known to the Author since his boyhood.

Other Books by Karl Keating

Debating Catholicism Series:

The Bible Battle

High Desert Showdown

Tracking Down the True Church

Face Off with an Ex-Priest

Debating Catholicism (four books in one)

How to Fail at Hiking Series:

How to Fail at Backpacking

How to Fail at Hiking Mt. Whitney

How to Fail at Hiking Yosemite

How to Fail at Hiking Grand Canyon

How to Fail at Hiking (four books in one)

Sun, Storm, and Solitude: Discovering Hidden Italy on the Cammino di San Benedetto

The Francis Feud

The New Geocentrists

Apologetics the English Way

Jeremiah's Lament

Anti-Catholic Junk Food

No Apology

The Ultimate Catholic Quiz

What Catholics Really Believe

Catholicism and Fundamentalism

Made in United States
Troutdale, OR
12/16/2023

16008144R00080